# THE OFFICIAL
# CRITICISM
# MANUAL

## Perfecting the Art of
## Giving and Receiving Criticism

☐

# DR. DEBORAH BRIGHT

*This book would not have been possible without the many contributions of my husband, Paul: my first, best, most loving, and most helpful critic.*

Seventh Printing

ISBN 0-9635783-08

# Preface

- In the face of today's information explosion, it is amazing to discover that the subject of criticism has been neglected. Few organizations address criticism as a specific topic within their core training curriculum, and even fewer understand how the subject is linked to motivation, increased productivity, and the development of quality relationships.

*The Official Criticism Manual* will help fill this void and will give a difficult subject a fresh look. The book is specially designed to enable the user to get needed information quickly and easily. Concepts and ideas are presented in a concise and to-the-point manner. The Table of Contents and the headings on each page will lead you quickly to the topics you need.

Keep this manual within easy access at home and at work. There is no place where quality criticism cannot be used to enhance your personal and professional relationships.

## ACKNOWLEDGMENTS

I owe a special thanks to a number of individuals who helped make this book what it is: to Bill Byler, my deep appreciation for its design; to Dawn Melley, my gratitude for its quality editing; to Deb Batterman, my profound thanks for her editorial guidance; and last but not least, I am forever grateful for the work and contributions of my loyal assistant, Rowena Chua.

DEBORAH BRIGHT

January 1991

# IN ADDITION TO OUR BOOK . . .

Dr. Deborah Bright offers consulting services, designs and delivers keynote presentations, workshops, seminars, and licensed programs specializing in subject areas including:

### Individual Performance Development

- **Turning Your Stress Into High Energy Performance**
- **Using Your Emotions as an Asset**
- **Performing Under Pressure**

### Management and Leadership Skills

- **Leading in the Decade Ahead: What's Different, What's Critical**
- **Coaching Others for Exceptional Performance**
- **Getting Employees to Achieve . . . Not Accomplish**

### Enhanced Communications

- **Fostering Open Communications: Tapping the Positive Power of Criticism**
- **Building Quality Communications in Teams and Work Groups**

For information on how Dr. Deborah Bright and her associates can help you and your organization, write or call:

**Bright Enterprises, Inc.**
**915 Broadway, Suite 1209**
**New York, NY 10010**
**(212) 533-5733**
**FAX (212) 533-7166**

# Table of Contents

**Introduction**                                                    ix

CHAPTER 1
**Understanding Criticism: Smashing the Myths**                     1

Myths: Criticism Can Be Positive • Criticism Cannot
Be Used as a Motivator • Personalizing Criticism Can
Be Avoided • Constructive Criticism Is Appreciated
• Givers Control the Criticism Process • It's Harder
to Receive Criticism Than to Give It • Always
Start With the Positive • Use "We," Not "You" •
Criticism Is Bad Because It Hurts • Employees Do
Not Want Criticism

CHAPTER 2
**Building a Strong Relationship**                                  11

Importance of Employee Expectation Packages •
Steps to Follow in Building Expectation Packages •
Identifying Unspoken Expectations • Communicating
Unspokens • Building a Common Understanding •
Keeping Agreements • How to Prevent Receiver
From Interpreting Criticism as Rejection

CHAPTER 3
**How to Deliver Quality Criticism: The Importance of
Being Prepared**                                                    21

Knowing Essential Information • Essential
Preparation Steps • Reflecting on Purpose of Criticism

• Knowing the Corrective Action Desired • Relating Examples Directly to Criticism • Handling an Urgent Need for Delivery of Criticism • Considering What You Know About Receiver, or Probing • Assessing Receiver's Capability to Change Behavior • Understanding Receiver's Criticism Preference • Keeping Criticism in Bounds • Rehearsing Delivery of Criticism • Explaining How to Take Appropriate Action • Using Appropriate Language and Concept Levels • Showing Value Behind Criticism • Explaining Why You Are Qualified to Give Criticism

## CHAPTER 4

### Overcoming Common Difficulties When Giving Criticism: What Do You Do When...?                                    45

Handling the Receiver Who Starts to Cry • Handling the Explosive Personality • Handling Those Who Deflect Criticism • Handling Those Who Fail to Take Corrective Action • Handling Unwillingness to Admit Errors • Handling Hurt Feelings

## CHAPTER 5

### Responding to Criticism as the Receiver: Using Control Effectively                                    53

Screening the Giver • Understanding What Is Being Said • Viewing Criticism as in Bounds • Examining the Criticism • Recognizing Supporting Examples • Clarifying Desired Action • Recognizing Positive Intent • Examining Alternatives and Consequences • Assessing Capability of Taking Desired Action • Avoiding Putting Personal/Mutual Interests in Jeopardy

  • Understanding Value of Desired Action  • Buying
Into Criticism

## CHAPTER 6
### Overcoming Common Difficulties When Receiving Criticism: What Do You Say, and When? 69

How to React to a String of Criticisms  • How to React
to "Hit and Run" Criticism  • How to React to Hyped-
Up or Exaggerated Criticism  • Handling Criticism in
Public  • Handling Criticism for Doing What You Were
Told to Do

## CHAPTER 7
### Quality Criticism: A Subtle Ingredient of Well-Functioning Teams 79

Criticism and Teamwork  • Making Criticism Part of a
Routine Day  • Letting the Leader's Role Be Known  •
Promoting Mutual Responsibility  • Establishing and
Enforcing Team Rules of Etiquette  • Creating an
Open Atmosphere

## CHAPTER 8
### A Word on Self-Criticism 89

Defining Self-Criticism  • Forms of Self-Criticism  •
Procrastination as a Form of Self-Criticism  •
Becoming a Real-Time Self-Criticizer  • Listening to
Your Self-Criticism  • Validating Self-Criticism  •
Assessing Proper Action  • Letting Go of Bad Feelings
  • Putting Worry and Guilt in Perspective

APPENDIX A   **Relationship Expectation Model**                                    105

APPENDIX B   **Giver Eloquence Questionnaire**                                     115

APPENDIX C   **Giver Action Plan**                                                 121

APPENDIX D   **Goal Sheet for Perfecting the Giving Criticism**                    127

# Introduction

■ Learning to handle criticism is a skill, and this book will develop your skills in giving and receiving criticism, as well as in dealing with self-criticism. Learning to unleash the positive force inherent in criticism helps you to communicate more honestly with others. The positive force found in criticism also fosters feelings of strength and confidence. As a result, it will be easier for you to remain open and objective when examining criticism received from others.

Giving quality criticism requires eloquence—an eloquence many people lack. Developing eloquence in giving criticism takes time and careful preparation, and one of the most indispensable tools you will ever have at your disposal is the "giver methodology chart" introduced in Chapter 3. By following the step-by-step process outlined in the chart you will learn to organize your thoughts and direct your energies productively, thus eliminating the sleepless nights and indigestion you may have experienced when agonizing over how best to deliver criticism. Answering each of the questions in the giver methodology chart will go a long way toward ensuring that the criticism is received as you intend it and that it will be positively acted upon.

Receiving criticism, like giving criticism, requires skill. In particular, receivers of criticism need to learn how to sort out the intentions behind the criticism and to minimize the tendency to personalize what is being said. That's where the "receiver control chart" introduced in Chapter 5 comes into play. With regular use of the chart you will be able to interpret criticism properly when you are on the receiving end and respond in a way that fosters a positive outcome.

Are you hard on yourself? In all likelihood, your answer is "yes." In fact, you're probably harder on yourself than you are on others. But self-criticism does not have to be an exercise in self-bashing. Chapter 8 will show how to productively handle self-criticism. In this chapter you will learn specific techniques that help you to become empowered and energized, not demoralized, from self-criticism.

Criticism touches each of us, and there's no way to avoid it. It is hoped that after reading this manual, a familiar subject will take on a fresh perspective.

## HOW TO USE THIS MANUAL

This manual is intended to be used as a reference. Store it within handy range. For easy access to information, refer to the detailed Table of Contents, which will point you to the important skill sets and issues you may need help with. Following are some tips to maximize the value to be gained from using this manual.

- When referring to either the giver methodology chart (Chapter 3) or the receiver control chart (Chapter 5), have specific examples in mind. This will make using both charts a little easier.

- If giving criticism is your primary area of interest, you may first want to complete the giver eloquence questionnaire in Appendix B. It will help you to determine how eloquently you deliver criticism. You might also consider re-examining your giver eloquence at a later date to help you note the progress you are making.

- You may find it helpful to bring this manual with you whenever you have to deliver criticism. During the exchange, both you and the person to whom you are delivering criticism can refer to the giver methodology chart and the receiver control chart to help ensure that quality criticism is communicated. Remember, few employees have ever received any formal training on how to receive criticism. The receiver control chart is designed to help them.
- If you are encountering an emotionally charged situation where you have to deliver criticism, the "giver action plan" in Appendix C will help you to sort things out. The plan gives you a series of questions to answer in order to help direct your energies in a productive way. As a result, you will more clearly understand the issue(s) at hand and how best to approach the individual.

## CHAPTER 1

# Understanding Criticism: Smashing the Myths

---

### Situation

The manager of a word-processing pool at a securities firm calls Lisa, one of her employees and a top-notch word processor, into her office. After Lisa sits down, the manager gets right to the point. "Lisa," she begins, "you've been overhearing a lot of talk about pending organizational changes here and I understand that you've been fueling the grapevine. What I called you in here for is to give you some advice. We are going through some rough times. Things are volatile. Top management is looking at everything. If you want to look good while all this is happening and possibly advance, then be careful about whom you talk to and what you say. Nothing is concrete—changes are in the discussion phase—and there may be political considerations in deciding who moves to what position."

"Are you telling me that I may not get a promotion?" Lisa asks.

"What I'm saying is that your eagerness may work against you," her manager continues. "And if I were you, I'd make a point of not being a part of the rumor mill."

### Question

Is this advice? Or is it criticism couched as advice?

■ Criticism is a familiar subject, but little attention is given to understanding it and even less time is devoted to learning how to handle it with eloquence. Surveys of over 3,000 employees throughout the nation indicate that only a small percentage have ever received any formal training in criticism.[1] Take yourself as an example. How eloquently do

---

[1] Bright Enterprises, "National Criticism Study" (New York 1989).

you handle criticism? Have you or the people you work with ever taken courses or workshops on the subject? Do you know that giving criticism is a skill (as is receiving it) and needs to be learned, much like golf or any other technique?

The workplace is fertile ground for everyday criticism. After tasks are assigned, for example, what is the boss supposed to do if the work is not completed properly? How can a manager develop employees if criticism is not communicated openly and clearly? During performance reviews, how can the boss communicate an honest profile about an employee's performance if criticism is not part of the appraisal process?

But what exactly is involved in effective criticism? Is criticism always negative? Can it be used as a motivational force, much like praise? Is it an important ingredient in building trust and enhancing teamwork? Who is in control when criticism is being communicated?

These questions and others will be addressed as we sort out the myths surrounding criticism and give a fresh perspective to a familiar subject.

## Myth 1: Criticism Can Sometimes Be Positive

In an era when "be more sensitive to others" and "seek personal fulfillment" have become catchphrases, criticism is often labeled an objectionable, even unmentionable, word. Consequently, many organizations try to disguise criticism by calling it something else—constructive confrontation, constructive criticism, positive feedback. Criticism at its core, however, will never be positive and never was intended to be, and employees are quick to see through the name changes. So let's start from a more realistic assumption: Criticism *is* negative. To try to hide that fact only results in deception. However, when used properly and when sometimes mixed with praise, criticism is an important ingredient in creating fine-tuned performance and maintaining consistently high levels of productivity. It's the proper balancing of criticism and praise that leads to improved performance and becomes what many managers refer to as the "gyroscope of guidance."

## Myth 2: Criticism Cannot Be Used as a Motivator

Many managers believe that the only way to successfully motivate others is through praise. This belief was encouraged by the work of Abraham H. Maslow, Frederick Herzberg, and other motivational theorists who stress praise as a motivator and make very little reference to the value of criticism. Let's take this belief to an extreme. What would happen if a manager relied exclusively on praise? In all likelihood, the praise would lose value and mean very little to the employees receiving it. Alternately, those receiving the praise may develop egos that become very difficult to deal with. Finally, the overuse of praise creates the possibility that standards of performance become lower than is desirable— something potentially devastating to the organization.

The typical manager, however, doesn't always praise. But when praise is used as a motivator, it is met with little or no resistance. The person receiving praise is not expected to change behavior but is encouraged to continue along on the particular course of action for which he has been praised.

Criticism, on the other hand, implies a change in behavior and is typically met with resistance. No wonder the giver of criticism goes through so much anguish before delivering it! But the effort is generally well worth it. Some experts, in fact, consider criticism the most powerful communication tool managers have at their disposal. Pointing out the negative aspects of a person's actions can lead to new challenges along with greater opportunities to succeed and perform at higher levels. For example, while a coach is criticizing an athlete during a practice session, the athlete is learning—learning how to do things better. That's motivating!

Not all criticism, however, is meant to be motivating. Sometimes it's used to hurt, embarrass, destroy, mentally paralyze, or get revenge. Whatever the purpose of criticism, its impact is extremely powerful, and it is this power that needs to be harnessed and directed in productive ways.

*Caveat:* Just as consistently praising others can lead to undesirable outcomes, so can overdoses of criticism. Used properly, it is motivating. Handled poorly, it can destroy a person's self-image and totally rattle his confidence. To sustain optimum performance over an extended period of time, remember that criticism needs to be properly balanced with praise.

### Myth 3: Personalizing Criticism Can Be Avoided

Many of us have been told, either informally or formally, to avoid criticizing the individual and to focus on the behavior. By focusing on the individual's behavior, the giver of criticism hopes to minimize hurt feelings.

> If there is anything "constructive" to the process
> of giving and receiving criticism, it's the outcome

In the best of all possible worlds, givers would subscribe to this practice. However, distinguishing the person from the behavior gets confusing when the giver has to approach the individual about issues such as hygiene or dress. The giver may choose all the right words to ensure that his message is framed in behavioral terms, but there's no getting around it: The more personal the issue, the harder it is to detach the person from the behavior.

### Myth 4: People Look Forward to Constructive Criticism

In the workplace, criticism is commonly referred to as constructive criticism. Perhaps the terms "constructive criticism" and "positive feedback" emerged as attempts to soften the negativity of criticism, but the terms are misleading. In fact, "constructive criticism" is an oxymoron—a combination of words that negate each other's meaning.

If there's anything constructive to the process of giving and receiving criticism, it's the *outcome*. In other words, after hearing the negative (i.e., criticism), a person wants the opportunity to do something about it that will eventually lead to a positive result. So, it isn't the criticism people look forward to—it's the positive, or constructive, outcome.

### Myth 5: The Giver Is in Control of the Criticism Process

Giving quality criticism requires thought. The giver has to think about what change in the receiver's behavior is desired and how criticism will bring about that change.

Because the giver initiates criticism, it is tempting to believe that the giver is in control of the criticism process.

On the contrary, it is the receiver who is in control. Why? Because the receiver does not have to take the criticism passively. The receiver can—and often does—challenge the giver. Receivers can challenge givers by asking for specific examples of behavior being criticized, or they can completely reject what is being said. And, it is the receiver who ultimately decides whether to accept the criticism by taking action to change a behavior pattern.

Where does the control lie for the giver? The giver is in control of the *preparation phase* of the criticism process, or that period of time prior to delivering the criticism when the giver can think through how best to approach delivering the criticism. And, as will be shown later, careful preparation is extremely important in assuring that the receiver will accept and positively act upon the criticism being presented.

## Myth 6: It's Harder to Receive Criticism Than to Give It

Because criticism is rooted in negativity, it's just as tough to give criticism as it is to receive it. Surveys have confirmed this: Givers claim that they are fearful of hurting the other person's feelings or are concerned that the criticism will not be received as intended. Receivers, on the others hand, find it difficult to avoid personalizing the criticism or reacting defensively. Many receivers question whether the giver still believes in them.

What we can learn from this insight is that engaging in a quality criticism exchange is a skill. Here are some questions to ask yourself as you develop that skill:

- How eloquently do you give criticism, and how receptive are you to receiving criticism?

- Is the relationship strengthened when you engage in the criticism exchange?
- Do both parties walk away sensing that there was honest communication and that things will improve because appropriate action will be taken?

### Myth 7: It's Best to Start With the Positive, Move to the Negative, and End With the Positive

Some training programs emphasize saying something positive before moving to the negative criticism and then ending the exchange on a positive note. There's a twofold purpose for using this "Oreo cookie" approach. First, starting and ending with the positive helps to soften the negative "blow." Second, starting with the positive theoretically creates a receiver who is more willing to listen to the criticism.

The problem with this approach is that it wrongly assumes that human beings are not complex and can easily be manipulated into accepting a three-step approach. Consequently, the manager who consistently uses the Oreo cookie approach may develop the reputation of being a "textbook communicator"—a reputation that can strip away respect.

Another problem is that this approach can easily backfire, especially if it is overused. The opening "positive" statement comes to mean very little to the receiver who knows it will be followed by a "but." Or, the receiver is so enamored with the positive that the criticism is never really heard or is taken lightly. Once again, the receiver is in control.

A similar approach advocated by some experts is to simply start with the positive before delivering the criticism. In this case, as with the Oreo cookie approach, the danger exists that the receiver may not hear the criticism, or their understanding of the criticism may be diminished because the praise is too distracting.

The popularity of beginning a criticism exchange on a positive note may be rooted in confusion over the difference between a critique and a criticism. Many people inaccurately use "critique" as a synonym for "criticism." In reality, these terms have different meanings. A critique is an evaluation of an entire piece of work. It examines positive as well as negative components. Criticism is the negative component of the critique. So, the close association between critique and criticism has confused many people into thinking that it's best to start off pointing out the positive when delivering criticism.

Beware of falling into the trap of always using the Oreo cookie approach to deliver criticism: Receivers may miss all or parts of the message. Managers, in particular, will be far ahead of the game when they recognize that sandwiching criticism between positive statements does little more than camouflage the real purpose of the criticism.

### Myth 8: Use "We," Not "You"

Management training programs repeatedly recommend handling confrontations by making reference to "we," not "you," throughout the exchange. Like the Oreo cookie approach, it's an attempt to soft-pedal the criticism.

Delivering criticism is not a "we" proposition. After all, it is the receiver who is being asked to change behavior. To begin by saying, for example, "we have a problem," is misleading. Therefore, in order to maintain credibility with the receiver, be direct: use "you."

## Myth 9: Criticism Hurts; Therefore, It Must Be Bad

Being on either the giving or receiving end of criticism is uncomfortable. The giver wants to avoid unintentionally hurting the receiver's feelings, and the receiver naturally feels uncomfortable when someone is pointing out something negative about her behavior. The discomfort does not mean that criticism is bad. On the contrary, quality criticism is intended to spur the receiver into action and to result in a positive outcome.

Because criticism is uncomfortable, it is especially important that the receiver keep hurt feelings in perspective and remember that the giver is simply communicating information. It is the receiver who colors what is being said. In fact, the worst thing a receiver can do is to stop listening because she feels hurt. Closing off information channels can be far more detrimental than suffering from the initial hurt.

## Myth 10: Employees Do Not Want to Be Critikized

On the contrary, employees want and expect criticism. When asked, they will invariably say that they want honest feedback from their bosses. They want to know what they are doing right and *what they are doing wrong*. But, while employees expect to be criticized by their bosses, they may resist the criticism because of "how" it is delivered.

## CHAPTER 2

# Building a Strong Relationship

---

*Situation*

The score is tied with only minutes left in the fourth quarter. The quarterback for the Washington Redskins makes a bad call and the play results in total confusion with no yardage gained. With a national television audience watching, the coach screams at the quarterback, who nods his head in agreement. Apparently unshaken, he runs back out to midfield and calls another play. Everything runs like clockwork. Not only do the Redskins get a much-needed first down, but the play also drives the ball into field goal range.

*Question*

How can a coach on national television scream at an athlete without creating feelings of resentment in the athlete? What makes the athlete go out on the playing field and perform better?

■  While the world of sports doesn't parallel the business world precisely, much can be learned from observing the interaction between a coach and an athlete. To begin with, the coach and his player share a common goal: winning. In business terms, winning translates into successful achievement of many goals. And a key component of success is building a good working relationship.

In sports, a good working relationship means the coach *can* criticize the athlete. In fact, the athlete expects criticism and is motivated by it. The same principle can be applied to the business environment.

How?

To increase performance and minimize confusion,
managers need to build "expectation packages"

In this chapter we will explore the importance of establishing mutually-agreed-upon expectations that help managers stimulate employees to do the best job they can.

## BUILDING EMPLOYEE EXPECTATION PACKAGES

In today's changing (and demanding) work environment, productivity concerns can be greatly reduced when managers and employees engage in communicating clear expectations. All too frequently, managers incorrectly assume that employees know their work assignments and how to work together as a team. This is especially true in environments characterized by rapid change, shifting priorities, and tremendous workloads. In this kind of environment, employees can easily become confused about what their duties exactly are and consequently fail to measure up to management expectations. To increase performance and minimize confusion, managers need to build "expectation packages."

An expectation package is exactly what it sounds like: those expectations discussed and mutually agreed upon by the manager and the employee. Creating the package involves clarifying expectations in four key areas: goals, work tasks, work quality, and the work relationship. Too often, instinct and assumptions take the place of clarified expectations. For example, although employees may know the goals of the department, they often are unaware of what part they are expected to play in achieving these goals or how the accomplishment of departmental goals contributes to achieving organizational goals. As a result, they make assumptions and do what they believe is expected of them, and if they're criticized for erring, they don't understand why. That's why communicating expectations is crucially important. Relying on instincts and assumptions may not always lead to a disastrous outcome, but it may subtly detract from building the type of working relationship and team spirit that contribute to exceptional performance.

Managers and employees both benefit when expectations are clarified at the outset for several reasons:

1. *Performance is heightened.*

   Because employees have a clear idea of what is expected of them, work gets done accurately and with quality—the first time.

2. *Energy is positively directed.*

   Instead of wasting precious energy guessing what is to be done or how to best work together, managers and employees are better able to direct their energies toward the successful completion of projects and assignments.

3. *There is a greater willingness to be more open and honest on the part of both managers and employees.*

   Praise and recognition are delivered with greater meaning and value. When errors do arise, criticism is better accepted and appropriate action is more likely to be taken.

4. *There is less of a need to criticize.*

   When you take the time up front to clearly express what you're asking others to do and to establish clear working relationships, misunderstandings, and therefore the need for criticism, occur less frequently. This is communicating and understanding expectations up front.

5. *The delegation process works.*

Mistakes are a given part of the business environment. Ironically, when they do occur, managers often obscure the delegation process by taking the task away from one person (especially if that person is defensive or difficult to deal with) and giving it to another. When shared expectations exist, however, the criticism is easily accepted and quickly acted upon. The employee enthusiastically returns to the task at hand. Thus, the delegation process is strengthened.

## HOW TO BUILD EXPECTATION PACKAGES

Managers are fooling themselves if they think their employees possess some instinctual sense of understanding about what is expected or desired. While instincts have their place in the manager-employee relationship, it is far better to engage in openly establishing clear expectations. Achieving congruency of expectations can best be done by engaging in a four-step process.

### Step 1: Identifying Unspoken Expectations

Unspoken expectations are the unstated "shoulds" and assumptions in the work relationship. For instance, managers may think that employees should, without recognition, always put out a 110 percent effort and should openly admit mistakes, take initiative, and voluntarily keep their bosses informed. Employees, on the other hand, may operate with the assumption that if they do good work, their bosses should take notice and recognize their efforts accordingly. And if they should err on a task, their boss would never openly criticize them in front of others. Such unspokens need to be identified so that little time and energy are wasted over guessing how things should be done and whether they are being done accurately, on time, and generally to everyone's satisfaction. Here's a classic example of what can happen when unspokens are not addressed. An employee who is frequently praised by her manager believes she's entitled to more money. When she doesn't get a salary increase, she becomes disgruntled. But if the unspoken expectations surrounding praise and reward had been identified, the employee would not have equated the compliments from her boss with remuneration.

### Step 2: Communicating Unspokens

Once unspoken expectations have been identified, they need to be communicated effectively, thus converting them to spoken expectations. The best way to clarify expectations is to begin by asking questions. During an informal conversation, for example, a manager might ask an employee: "Putting money aside, how can I best acknowledge your work when it is above and beyond what is expected?" Or: "If you make a mistake, how can I let you know so that it's not taken the wrong way?" While this may seem a very time-consuming way to uncover information, the value to be gained in terms of increased productivity and morale will far outweigh the initial time investment.

### Step 3: Building a Common Understanding

Expectation packages will have little or no meaning if managers and employees do not first establish a clear understanding of how best to work together. People bring different styles to the way they work. These differences need to be acknowledged. Managers and employees need to develop mutual respect for each other's way of working if there is to be a foundation of trust.

Whether done formally or informally, building this mutual understanding is rarely done in one hour or in one minute, as a popular book might suggest! Rather, it's more of an ongoing exchange. As one manager said, "When I first interview employees, we discuss a number of expectations; however, I have overlooked the importance of keeping up this practice. God knows our lives make drastic changes, so I can see how valuable it is to periodically go back and update certain expectations." This is valuable advice.

### Step 4: Keeping Agreements

The solidifying step to building the expectation package is keeping agreements. Obviously, both parties need to keep agreements. However, it is the boss's responsibility to manage the agreement. When the expectation package is put into practice, the relationship begins to form roots. The relationship will continue to grow and stay healthy only if trust through keeping agreements remains consistent.

## ADDRESSING THE RECEIVER'S UNSPOKEN EXPECTATION: REJECTION

Often, an unspoken feeling that many receivers of criticism cling to when the boss is criticizing them is: "He no longer believes in me." Or they may think: "I've blown it. Will he ever see me in the same light?" Or: "She will never trust me again," "He's lost faith in me," "I've ruined my chances for any kind of promotion." In each case, the employee is interpreting the criticism as a sign of rejection and making a giant leap in logic that needs some quick clarification.

Ensuring that the receiver interprets the criticism as simply pointing out a mistake and nothing more requires special attention on the part of the giver. Outlined below are six effective approaches.

1. *Use signals.*

   Sending a mutually understood and accepted signal certainly helps to reassure the receiver that everything is okay and the discussion is only about an error. For example, on the football field after a quarterback mishandles a play, you'll notice team members patting the quarterback as if to say, "All is well, stay in there, we believe in you!" A similar signal can be easily conveyed between a manager and his employees. Signals can go a long way toward nurturing trust—the glue of quality relationships.

2. *Give the person a similar or more difficult task.*

   Actions speak louder than words. When a manager tells an employee a mistake she made is "no big deal" and then gives her assigned task to someone else, the employee understandably feels that the manager doesn't believe in her. One surefire way to let receivers know you believe in them is to let them continue on the same assignment or give them one that is even slightly more complex.

3. *Express your belief in the person.*

   A simple verbal message of "I believe in you" works and sometimes is all that is necessary.

4. *Engage the employee in a conversation and really listen when he speaks.*

   Asking for input and listening to responses helps to minimize defensiveness. At the same time, you're letting the employee know you believe in him.

5. *Talk about something off-the-job.*

   After the criticism has been delivered, bringing up something off-the-job helps to ease tensions. It lets employees know that to be criticized is simply a matter of doing one's work. This approach helps to keep criticism in its proper perspective.

6. *Throw away the criticism.*

   Sometimes receivers get concerned about whether the criticism will unexpectedly resurface one or two weeks later from now at a staff meeting or later on in their performance review. The following technique can eliminate this concern while simultaneously reassuring the receiver that it's time to direct energies in a productive way. On a piece of paper, note the situation in question. When the discussion is over, take the piece of paper and crumple it up before tossing it into the wastepaper basket. Give some closing remark to remove all doubt about your actions such as, "Now let's go forward from here," or "This situation is behind us. Let's move forward and remember the lesson but not the mistake." Besides eliminating fears in the receiver about possible future repercussions, this "wastepaper basket" technique is a helpful reminder for the giver to avoid carrying any bias against the receiver. (The wastepaper basket technique qualifies as a "quick charge," which are mental and physical techniques usable on-the-spot for regaining self-control and for better handling difficult situations. Other quick charges are introduced later in this book.)

## CONCLUSION

Any meaningful relationship has as its foundation a clearly established expectation package. The four-step process discussed in this chapter is an effective way to build expectation packages.

Going through this process takes time and involves a certain degree of flexibility and understanding on the part of both parties. It is important to recognize that the expectation package needs to be updated periodically, because people's lives change and so will their expectations. Keeping the expectation package current can be easily accomplished by engaging in a conversation either during a formal meeting (e.g., a performance review) or an informal meeting (e.g., a coffee break).

When expectations are clearly communicated and understood, there is little need to criticize. So, rather than promoting criticism, promote establishing expectation packages. After all, expectation packages are the architect's blueprint to building strong relationships.

## CHAPTER 3

# How to Deliver Quality Criticism: The Importance of Being Prepared

### Situation

Charlie is the district manager for a profitable insurance company in Stamford, Connecticut. Helen, an agent who has been with the company for four years, is not having a good year. Charlie knows he has to talk to Helen about the difficulties she is experiencing, and for the past two nights he has anguished over how best to deal with her. Well known to Charlie is Helen's tendency to become hysterical whenever negative aspects of her performance are addressed. He knows that if he approaches her the wrong way, the matter could become worse instead of better.

### Question

Charlie knows what he must do; what advice could you offer him on how he should deliver his criticism?

■    This chapter will introduce a valuable tool for delivering criticism—the giver methodology chart. The chart logically sequences what a giver needs to think about and subsequently know in order to ensure that the criticism is received as intended and that proper action follows. But even before a giver can take the steps outlined in the chart, he should know certain things about the receiver and their relationship.

## KNOW ESSENTIAL INFORMATION

Prior to thinking through how to approach Helen, Charlie needs to consider whether he's properly prepared. Being properly prepared involves considering three essential things:

1. *Know the mutual and individual goals.*

   An integral part of the expectation package is the establishment of mutual and individual goals. When goals are not understood, it's difficult to present the criticism as having any value, and the giver's intention may be questioned. As a result, the receiver may be more likely to reject the criticism. Invest time in knowing the employee's goals and be sure that the employee and you mutually agree that they square with those of the organization.

2. *Know the individual's criticism preferences.*

   Managers truly committed to developing their people will find that using criticism is inescapable. It's part of doing business, just like getting projects completed on time. Rather than guessing how best to approach individual players on your team, managers need to be aware of how they prefer being approached. Some may prefer a direct approach while others may prefer a softer, more cushioned approach. The best way to find out is to ask. It's that simple.

3. *Examine your own personal impressions and thoughts.*

   Your personal impressions of an individual will gravely affect your approach to criticism. When dealing with people who are not on your "favorite" list, some extra effort to remain open-minded when delivering the criticism is called for. Otherwise, you may fall into the trap of unfairly believing the receiver is incapable of change and inadvertently conveying that. Giving people permission to change—regardless of whether you like them—is a key component of being an outstanding coach, parent, or manager. On the other hand, liking the person you need to criticize doesn't necessarily make things any easier. Difficulties arise when you become fearful of hurting the other person's feelings or in some way damaging the relationship.

Back to Charlie. Let's assume that he has equipped himself for dealing with Helen. He has worked with her for some time and knows her goals and her criticism preference; but he still finds himself anguishing over how best to communicate the criticism.

Ironically, Charlie's anguish is a good sign: It means that he's trying to think through and organize his thoughts about how to best approach her. He's aware that as the giver, once you deliver criticism, control shifts to the receiver. So what can Charlie do to help ensure that his dialogue with Helen will be productive and result in a positive outcome? He can refer to the giver methodology chart (see pages 24 and 25).

The giver methodology chart is used during the preparation phase to help ensure that quality criticism is delivered and to help the giver think through how to logically handle the criticism by asking a series of core questions. If any of these core questions is overlooked, the criticism is at risk of either being rejected, proving ineffective, or causing the relationship to suffer irreparable damage.

The core questions are sequenced below in three steps. Answering the core questions from each of the steps helps to properly position the criticism so that it will lead to the desired productive outcome. A "yes" response swiftly moves you along to the next question or step. An "unsure" or a "no" response may cause you to question the purpose of the criticism or direct you back to the receiver for additional

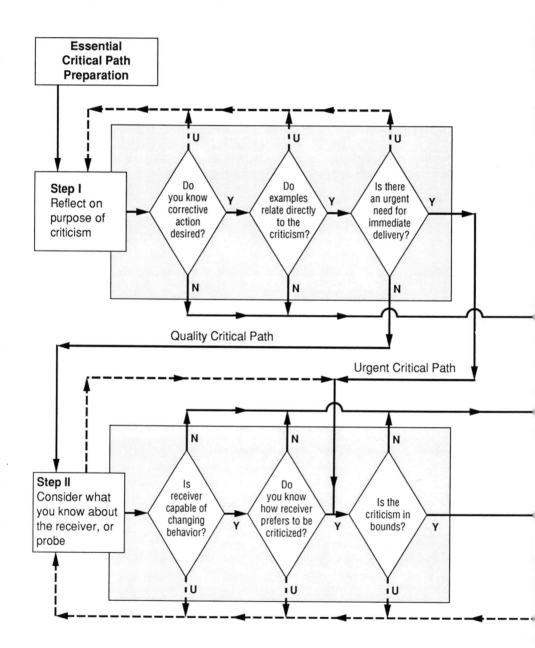

**Essential Critical Path Preparation**

**Step I**
Reflect on purpose of criticism

U — Do you know corrective action desired?
Y

U — Do examples relate directly to the criticism?
Y

U — Is there an urgent need for immediate delivery?
Y

N

N

N

Quality Critical Path

Urgent Critical Path

**Step II**
Consider what you know about the receiver, or probe

N — Is receiver capable of changing behavior?
Y

N — Do you know how receiver prefers to be criticized?
Y

N — Is the criticism in bounds?
Y

U

U

U

Y = Yes
N = No
U = Unsure

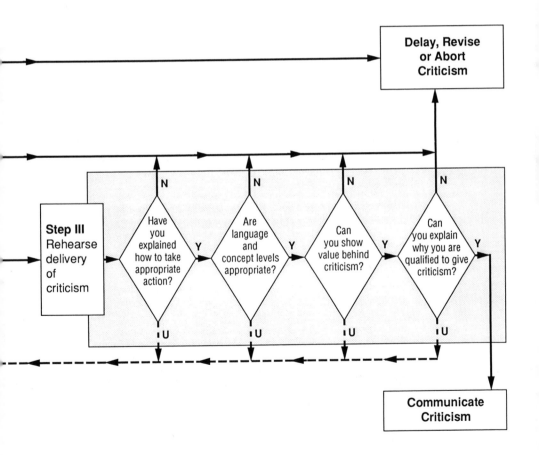

Delay, Revise
or Abort
Criticism

**Step III**
Rehearse
delivery
of
criticism

N — Have you explained how to take appropriate action? — Y

N — Are language and concept levels appropriate? — Y

N — Can you show value behind criticism? — Y

N — Can you explain why you are qualified to give criticism? — Y

U     U     U     U

**Communicate Criticism**

information. *If you are unable to satisfactorily answer any question, it is advisable to revise, delay, or abort the criticism.*

## ESSENTIAL CRITICAL PATH PREPARATION

As you approach Step I of the giver methodology chart, you will be initiating a sequence of logic that moves along the essential critical path. Moving along the path from question to question and step to step will bring you increasingly closer to ensuring that the criticism is valid and that positive action can be taken. As each question is mentally answered, the giver is properly positioning the criticism so that it will lead to a productive outcome.

Keep in mind that urgent situations may arise that make it difficult to stick to the entire critical path. The giver methodology chart addresses urgent situations by causing the giver to modify the essential critical path and jump from Step I to the last step, or Step III. Givers need to be aware when making this jump that the criticism is at greater risk of being rejected.

The essential critical path preparation directs the giver into thinking about the purpose behind the criticism. All questions in Step I address this very important focus.

## STEP I: REFLECT ON THE PURPOSE OF THE CRITICISM

Underlying the purpose of criticism is an intent to bring about a positive change in behavior. However, this intent oftentimes gets misdirected when givers fail to think before they speak. Here's a good example: A manager schedules a morning staff meeting to begin promptly at 9:30. One of his employees walks into the meeting at 9:42. The manager interrupts the meeting and hastily says, as the employee takes his seat, "Well, glad you could join us at 9:42..."

Now, what is the manager's purpose here? Obviously, it isn't to let the employee know that the manager can tell time. Indirectly, the manager may have been trying to convey to all present the importance of punctuality. All well and good—however, the method used risked creating a relationship crisis that could far outweigh the value of making the point.

Here's another familiar situation where the intention behind the criticism is potentially misdirected. Jerry, the manager of an information management system group, gets a call from his boss. It seems that Tom, who is in Jerry's department, sent out project information to a client without first getting the necessary approval. The client became upset because his company had invested a significant amount of money in the project in question, and the information received was woefully inaccurate. When Jerry gets off the phone, he marches over to Tom's office and lets him have it.

JERRY: Tom, I can't believe you did this!

TOM: Did what?

JERRY: Never send anything to the Jericho people until it has the right approvals! Now I've got *my* boss on the phone yelling at me because *you* screwed up. I can't believe it! When you are careless like this, Tom, you make me look bad. You're going to have to stay here tonight and get this thing fixed. I don't care what it takes. I hate looking dumb in front of my boss.

Let's briefly examine this dialogue for how it measures up to what we have been discussing.

Was Jerry's purpose for giving the criticism clear? Are there any indications that Jerry even communicated clearly to Tom exactly what "right approvals" means? Did Jerry show any sensitivity to how Tom prefers to be criticized?

The answer to all the above is no. In fact, Tom may never have been told what approvals were necessary. Also, he may never have realized what an important unspoken not "looking dumb" in front of the boss was to Jerry. Jerry put at risk his relationship with Tom—unnecessarily and perhaps for a very long time.

In order to ensure that the purpose of the criticism is to bring about a positive outcome, you need to consider if corrective action is possible and, if so, ask:

■ ### Do you know the corrective action desired?

Too often we let our emotions overpower us and blurt out things that give us momentary relief but leave behind a wake of bad feelings. For example, let's say that one of your employees keeps asking trite questions or the kind of questions she should be able to answer for herself. You finally lose your composure and say something like: "You keep interrupting me with these stupid questions. Gosh, you are so dumb!" Criticism of this kind is rarely intended to help the receiver take action. Instead, its purpose is destructive. It may momentarily relieve you (the giver), but in the long run it will create possibly irreparable bitter feelings. Typically, productivity will suffer and team spirit will ebb.

On the other hand, if you had taken a moment to think about the specific action you wanted from the receiver, you may not have responded the way you did. Knowing the corrective action desired prior to delivering the criticism helps you to quickly sort out the purpose of the criticism. For instance, if no action can be taken, either abort, delay, or revise the criticism. If you are unsure about what action the receiver can take, then re-examine the purpose of your criticism. For criticism to bring about a positive outcome, the specific desired action must be known.

The positive intent of the criticism can be overshadowed when the criticism lacks validity. One way to ensure the validity of the criticism is for the giver to ask himself:

■ ### *Do examples relate directly to the criticism?*

When no specifics are presented, receivers start to question whether the giver took any time to understand the circumstances surrounding the criticism. For instance, when a giver says, "From what I can see you're not playing on the team," the receiver is going to want some specifics to help better understand what he is doing wrong. If the giver cannot provide specifics, the receiver is apt to become suspicious of the purpose behind the criticism and less willing to take appropriate action.

Having specific examples may not be enough, however, to ensure acceptance of the criticism. It is crucial to examine whether the examples relate directly back to the criticism. For example, a boss gets a letter back from his secretary. He notices that there are two misspellings in the letter. One of them is the client's name. The boss is infuriated and yells at the secretary for the misspellings.

The secretary can't understand why the boss is getting so upset over two typographical errors. Yet if you were to question the boss about what really made him so angry, he might say it was his secretary's lack of attention to detail and the absence of pride in her work—two important messages that never got communicated.

Sometimes problems arise when it is necessary to take urgent action. The urgency of a situation will help determine the purpose of the criticism. To properly position the criticism, it is important to ask:

■ ***Is there an urgent need for immediate delivery?***

Sometimes circumstances are such that it is necessary to take urgent action. You're in a crisis—if you don't criticize the appropriate people, valuable time will be lost and the company will suffer financially. Or you are visiting your staff out in the field, and if you don't say something now while you are face to face with them, it will be three months before you meet with them again.

These are just two legitimate circumstances when it is impractical to delay or abort the criticism. If you find that there is an urgent need to criticize, then move directly to the "urgent critical path" sequence of questions, where you mentally rehearse your delivery of the criticism before communicating it. The first urgent question to ask yourself is whether the criticism is in bounds. This is an important consideration because it forces you to examine whether expectations have been clearly communicated from the onset. If the answer to this question is not conclusive, then it will be necessary for you to revise the delivery of the criticism; otherwise, you run the risk of having the criticism rejected and finding the receiver unwilling to take appropriate and timely action.

After determining whether the criticism is in bounds, the urgent critical path moves you directly to Step III, where you mentally rehearse your delivery of the criticism before communicating it. Each of the questions in Step III will be elaborated on later in this chapter. For now, keep in mind that answering the questions raised in Step III will not interfere with the immediacy of the situation—you will do it at lightning speed.

*Caveat:* When you believe there is an urgent need to deliver criticism, you are letting that need outweigh other important considerations that help to bring about the delivery of quality criticism and ensure its acceptance. If, after examining whether there is an urgent need to deliver criticism you are *unsure*, then reassess your purpose for criticizing.

If you believe there is no urgent need to criticize, then move to the "quality critical path" series of questions. Thinking about the quality critical path shifts your attention from the criticism itself to consideration of the receiver. Here, you will be mentally asking yourself questions about how the receiver will perceive the criticism and what it will take for you to engage the receiver in accepting and acting upon the criticism. Answering these questions accurately will ensure that quality criticism is delivered and that positive results will occur.

## STEP II: CONSIDER WHAT YOU KNOW ABOUT THE RECEIVER, OR PROBE

Because of the negativity associated with criticism, receivers can be particularly sensitive. As a result, receivers are often not only focusing on what is being said but are alert to the circumstances surrounding how and when the criticism is delivered. Besides the receiver rejecting the criticism, the quality of the relationship may be damaged if the giver has not considered the receiver's capacity for change or criticism preference. So, the giver needs to ask:

■ *Is the receiver capable of changing behavior?*

When considering each of the questions in Step II, keep in mind that if you are unsure about an answer, the giver methodology chart directs you to consider what you know about the receiver and, when necessary, to probe further. This is an important consideration. Criticizing someone who cannot make the changes required only sets the receiver up for continued criticism.

An example will illustrate. Leo, owner and chief financial officer for a small business on the East Coast, is constantly criticizing his newly appointed manager, Hal, for not taking steps to keep up company morale. Hal had been Leo's star technician and Leo believed that Hal's appointment to a managerial position would be mutually beneficial. Hal, however, is simply not cut out for management, and becomes more and more demoralized by the criticism. Fortunately, Leo takes the time to look at the situation objectively and realizes he has fallen into the trap of seeing Hal as he wants him to be rather than who he really is.

## To build a constructive relationship, you must know how others prefer to be criticized

If you are unsure about a person's capabilities, go directly to the person and ask. This is what Marilyn does. Senior editor for a major women's magazine, Marilyn has an assistant, Josephine, who is continuously making grammatical errors. Marilyn points out the mistakes and when time permits she provides a short explanation. One day Marilyn decides to approach Josephine about the frustration she is experiencing in her efforts to get more accurate work. During their conversation, Josephine admits that her knowledge of grammar is weak. Their discussion concludes with a two-month improvement plan. Both agree that if satisfactory progress does not follow, Josephine is not suited for the job.

Knowing how best to approach the receiver can oftentimes make the difference as to whether the criticism is listened to, accepted, and acted upon. As discussed earlier, anyone interested in building a strong, productive relationship needs to know the other person's criticism preference. In order to ensure that quality criticism is delivered, the giver needs to ask:

■ *How does the receiver prefer to be criticized?*

The importance of knowing individual criticism preferences cannot be overemphasized. When you take into account how the receiver prefers to be criticized, it's valuable to consider time and place. For instance, some receivers prefer being criticized in the morning. They like having the chance to correct any problem immediately. Other people clearly prefer having the criticism delivered at the end of the day so they can think about it overnight. Others will lose sleep thinking about it overnight.

A good rule of thumb concerning place is: Don't criticize in public. This means within the company as well as outside of the work setting. Also, consider that some people prefer criticism in casual circumstances (during lunch, for example) while others have a strong preference for work-related criticism to be delivered at work. Besides addressing time and place preferences, it's important to give consideration to how the criticism is delivered. Receivers are not likely to be responsive to givers who yell or keep repeating the criticism as if to hammer it in. And using words like "selfish," "controlling," "aggressive," or "lazy" may easily distract the receiver and cause sparks to fly.

If you don't know an individual's criticism preference, delay delivering the criticism and ask the receiver a number of questions during a relaxed time. Some good questions are:

- Did you ever work really well with your boss? What made the relationship special?

- When you made a mistake, how would he handle it?

- Can you recall a boss who you really had a hard time working with? What about her made it so tough? How would she criticize you?

Other effective questions for eliciting information about an individual's criticism preference are:

- Between now and the end of the year, are you going to make a mistake? (If the answer is "yes," continue with: "Since we both agree that mistakes will arise, how can I best call attention to a mistake without it upsetting you or causing you to receive the criticism other than how it was intended?")

- I realize we have worked together for a while and all the time I've assumed that I know how best to communicate with you; but I thought it would be helpful if I asked you how you would like me to point out errors in your work without your misinterpreting what I am saying. And how can I let you know that I still believe in you?

There are times when criticism is rejected because the receiver simply is not in the proper frame of mind to listen to negative comments. Or, rejection of the criticism can occur because the receiver perceives the giver as out of line for reasons of content. The giver should ask:

■ ### *Is the criticism in bounds?*

The key boundaries involved in giving criticism are timing and content of the criticism. Let's first discuss timing.

Timing is important from the perspectives of both the giver and the receiver. If the giver is in a bad mood or is pressed for time, then delivering the criticism is momentarily out of bounds. If the receiver is depressed or sad, he may not be in the right frame of mind to act on the criticism.

If you are unsure about the timing, ask the receiver. Here's an example. John has been out of his office all day at meetings. When he returns, his assistant, Tom, hands him a report. There are several errors in the report. Rather than immediately criticizing Tom, John says, "Tom, I don't know what you've had to put up with all day, but I'd like to go over this report. There are some things that need to be changed. Is now a good time?"

The giver must also consider whether the content of the criticism is within the bounds of the relationship. Put another

## If criticism does not fit with mutually understood expectations, it may be rejected

way, does the criticism fit with the mutually understood goals of the giver and the receiver?

Sue, a secretary/receptionist, is usually very courteous when one of her boss's peers comments every morning on how nice she looks. One day, however, he comes by and criticizes the outfit she is wearing. Instead of being her usual polite self, she says, "Just because you think you can compliment me every day on the way I look doesn't give you the right to criticize me when my dress doesn't meet with your approval. I don't even report to you." In this case, the receiver declared that the criticism was out of bounds.

Relationships are surrounded by expectations. If you bring up something that is outside the parameters of the expectations established, then the criticism runs the risk of being rejected. Tasks also have certain expectations attached to them. If the criticism is delivered without the expectations clearly communicated up-front, the receiver will reject the criticism and will say instead, "I didn't know I was supposed to do it this way. No one ever told me." And that's valid.

If you are unsure about whether the expectations have been communicated, you might say to the receiver: "This is a clarification. Next time it will be a criticism." A simple statement like this can help ensure that the receiver doesn't reject the criticism as out of bounds. In this case, it is the giver who is establishing the boundaries of allowable criticism.

### STEP III: REHEARSE DELIVERY OF CRITICISM

After considering the critical questions, putting all the information together is what helps to ensure the delivery of quality criticism. Incorporating all of the information into the presentation of the criticism and coming across in a believable way is accomplished by mentally rehearsing the delivery of the criticism, which is addressed in Step III of the giver methodology chart. The questions asked in Step III are part of both the quality critical path and the urgent critical path. Including Step III as part of both paths stresses the importance of mental rehearsal. Let's explore the value to be gained from mentally rehearsing the delivery of criticism, through examining the questions raised in Step III.

Mental imagery and visualization techniques designed to enhance performance may be applied to delivering criticism. Rehearsing your delivery helps you to uncover subtle signs, such as a certain sigh or shifting of the eyes, that can cause the receiver to question your intentions. Rehearsing also helps to build your confidence and ensures that you deliver the criticism in the most effective way. You might rehearse timing, tone of voice, expression of delivery, focus, and control. Criticism that conveys guilt, disappointment, or even rejection can have an extremely negative outcome—be sure to check your delivery to exclude these nonproductive messages.

When mentally rehearsing your delivery of criticism, it is important that you consider and incorporate in your final delivery answers to the following questions.

■ ### Have you explained how to take appropriate action?

In Step I of the giver methodology chart, the giver must give thought to the desired action. At this point, it's valuable to offer the receiver specific insights into the desired action.

Doing so helps to instill confidence in the receiver. Remember, you want the receiver to walk away from the criticism with a good idea of what needs to be done to correct a situation.

Here's a typical situation. John reports to Mary. She thinks John has a "bad attitude" because whenever she introduces a new idea for enhancing certain efficiencies, John questions everything she says. But what good does it do John if Mary communicates to him that he has a "bad attitude"? It's not specific enough. She will elicit the desired behavior far more easily if she simply says to John, "Whenever we discuss new ideas for approaching a problem, rather than questioning the ideas, it would be helpful if you came up with alternatives to the ones suggested." Now John has a clearer idea of the specific desired behavior.

By thinking about and specifying what you want from receivers, you turn the criticism into a motivational tool for enhancing performance and building better relationships. What gets the receiver's attention is what you *want* more than what you said.

■ ### *Are language and concept levels appropriate?*

When practicing delivery, it is important to consider whether you are using language and concepts that will help the receiver understand your message. Here's a good example of how an executive successfully handled a very sensitive situation with somebody he happened to like a great deal:

Dave, who happens to be a fanatical Red Sox fan, was recently promoted into management and is having a difficult time making the transition. The job is demanding and he is overwhelmed with the fifteen people he manages. Recognizing the need to change Dave's position without his losing confidence or feeling that he is being demoted, the boss says, "Dave, we've played ball together for a long time, and you're known to be a good player. There are certain basics that a player has got to have. If a player doesn't have those basics, chances are slim that he'll ever be great at the game. Well, as a new manager who's got a full career ahead, you've got to have a chance to learn the basics of management. After all, in management as in baseball, if you don't have the basics from the beginning, it will hurt you in the long run. That's why I want to move you into a less hectic environment. You'll have a chance to manage fewer people, which will afford you the time needed to learn the basics."

Using appropriate concepts and language is extremely important today as the work force becomes more culturally diverse and as educational levels vary. Too often, we incorrectly assume that others know the meaning of words we use regularly in our departments or that are commonplace within our industry. One resourceful manager made a successful effort to speak to an employee about her lack of organization. The employee was unable to read and had very little schooling. Nevertheless, she was a loyal, hard worker. To help her understand the importance of being organized, he framed the criticism in terms of motherhood. He said: "A mother raising one child doesn't have to be quite as organized as a mother raising three children, but mothers who are organized can do their work easily." Because she comes from a large family, she can easily relate to what he is trying to get across.

## Link the person's goals to the criticism... and show value

■   *Can you show value behind the criticism?*

Before you deliver criticism, you need to be sure you know the answers to the following questions. If you can't answer any one of these questions, then you need to delay the criticism.

- Do you know the employee's short- and long-term goals?
- Have you discussed and mutually agreed upon departmental goals?
- Have you discussed quality and other expectations related to the situation at hand?

If you know the goals, then be sure to link them to the criticism. When you do this, you help to clarify the intention behind the criticism and you give a valuable reason for taking action. Adults are less apt to enthusiastically do something simply because someone tells them to. They prefer knowing what they can expect to gain.

Let's say you have an employee who dresses poorly. You might simply say to her: "You need to improve your dress." But don't be surprised if the employee does nothing. Unless you offer insights into what the employee can do to improve her dress, and what she can gain by doing so, the value of the criticism is missing. Here's the same criticism presented so it has value. "Marilyn, you said that you wanted to become a supervisor. Keep in mind that if you want to advance, there are some unspoken elements that you need to pay attention to, and dress is one of the unspoken elements. Well, if you want to be part of the management team, give some thought to dressing in a more acceptable way. Observe others. It is your visible commitment to being part of the team."

■    *Can you explain why you are qualified to give criticism?*

At this stage, it is important that you know exactly why you are qualified to deliver the criticism. The reason you consider this question last is that it is one of the first things the receiver is going to think about when the criticism is delivered.

If you answered "yes" to this question, you are properly prepared to proceed with delivering the criticism.

How do you know you are qualified to deliver the criticism? You are qualified if you are an authority figure and/or responsible for the final outcome of task projects. That includes bosses, project leaders, and parents. Another important factor in determining whether you are qualified is knowledge level. If the giver is highly knowledgeable in the area, the receiver is apt to accept and take action on the criticism. Other important factors include respect and trust. If, on the other hand, you have criticized the person several times before with no results, then you need to examine whether you are the best person to offer the criticism. You may have the authority to give the criticism, but you may not be the best person to do so because the relationship is strained owing to problems of respect and personality differences. Let's say one of your employees has trouble controlling his temper. Even though to criticize is within the bounds of the relationship, you may want an outside person, such as a consultant, to deal with that issue.

## CONCLUSION

The giver methodology chart will help you uncover important information necessary for delivering quality criticism. But putting your thoughts into words to initiate the criticism can sometimes seem awkward.

Keep in mind as you dwell on how to best deliver criticism that you are not alone. This is something that many people anguish over. Here are some tips to help you get over the hesitation.

- *Tell yourself to stay flexible.*
  Human beings are complex, so your approach will need to vary.

- *Create a comfortable atmosphere.*
  The setting you select will help to create the tone for the criticism (e.g., a conference room may set a formal tone; a restaurant will set an informal tone).

- *Getting started well is important.*
  If you feel that the criticism may cause the person to react in a defensive way or if you prefer to ease into the subject, then you might begin by reiterating and reconfirming the expectation package you mutually established. For instance, you might start off by saying, "One of the things we both value in our relationship is being honest with one another. Agreed?" Or, "You've asked me to tell you what you are doing wrong as soon as I become aware of it. Correct?" Asking the other person to acknowledge that she agrees provides the go-ahead needed to proceed. If you go to step II, you'll remember to consider the individual's criticism preference. If the receiver prefers that you get right to the point, then that's the best way to get started.

- *Relate to the goals of the receiver.*
  If you know what the person's goals are, you can open the discussion by restating the goals. Making analogies or using concepts that the receiver can easily relate to helps increase the understandability of the criticism and clarifies the intent. It may take days or even weeks to collect the information outlined in this chapter. As long as you are being conscientious, do not let this delay concern you. Because people are creatures of habit, chances are good that if they were making mistakes yesterday, they will make the same or similar mistakes tomorrow. It's up to you as the giver to present the criticism in such a way that the receiver will listen, understand, and want to take immediate action. To help you in preparing to deliver criticism, use the following checklist. It summarizes the procedures that were described in this chapter.

## GIVER CHECKLIST

Before delivering criticism, prepare yourself by answering each of the following questions:

**1.** Do you know the desired behavior?

**2.** Can you provide specifics?

**3.** Do the specifics relate directly to the criticism?

**4.** Is there an urgent need to deliver the criticism? (If the answer to this question is "yes," jump to question 8.)

**5.** Is the person capable of correcting what is being criticized?

**6.** Do you know how the person typically reacts to criticism?

**7.** Is the criticism in bounds?

**8.** Have you mentally rehearsed delivery of the criticism?

**9.** Are you using appropriate language in approaching the receiver?

**10.** Does the criticism fit in with mutual and individual goals?

**11.** Will the criticism be perceived as having value?

**12.** Are you qualified to deliver the criticism?

If the answer to all questions is "yes," move to the next step—deliver the criticism. If the answer to any question is "no," delay, revise, or abort the criticism. If you are unsure of an answer to any question, re-examine the purpose of the criticism or probe further.

## CHAPTER 4

# Overcoming Common Difficulties When Giving Criticism: What Do You Do When...?

*Situation*

Marilyn, an executive secretary, is called into her boss's office. Her boss is upset that Marilyn bypassed him in order to deal with a recent memo that came from corporate. Being reprimanded for this touches a sensitive nerve in Marilyn. She had never intended to offend her boss, she explains as her eyes well with tears.

*Question*

How should Marilyn's boss finesse the situation?

■ In preparing to give criticism, it's not enough to focus on the nature of the criticism. Givers need to give consideration to the human factor as well. This means having strategies for dealing with emotional outbursts or any number of difficult situations that may arise. This chapter will explore some of the more common difficulties givers encounter.

## Situation 1

What do you do when the receiver starts to cry?

Men and women cry for a variety of reasons, and it's dangerous to assume that crying is a reaction to hurt feelings. Oftentimes, receivers cry because of tremendous anger welling up inside. Regardless of the reason, tears are often uncontrollable and bound to make both the giver and receiver uncomfortable.

The "exit approach" is particularly effective when a receiver bursts out crying. For the giver, exiting, or momentarily leaving the scene, is a way of tactfully allowing the receiver to regain composure. It also demonstrates some sensitivity to the receiver. Receivers are frequently embarrassed by reactive outbursts. For that reason, it's a good practice for the giver to let the receiver know when he'll be back (say, in a few minutes). Providing a time frame reassures the receiver that the giver will return and provides them an opportunity to respond to the criticism.

### Situation 2

What do you do when you need to criticize a transfer from another area into your department who is known to be explosively interruptive and walks out whenever criticism is directed to him?

Even before giving criticism, referring to Step II of the giver methodology chart (see Chapter 3) will help prepare you for factoring in how the receiver can best respond to criticism. In this case, you already know the receiver is the explosive type, so you might try asking him during a casual exchange how to best work around his explosive behavior. One manager in this situation gets his explosive employee to agree that when emotions run high, the employee can excuse himself to get a drink of water and then return. For an entire year after making the agreement the employee needs to exit the situation only twice. And on each occasion the mutual respect and cooperation between employee and manager is very evident.

Another manager faced with this type of individual tries a less tactful approach: He quickly jumps from his seat and blocks the door to prevent the employee from leaving. They both laugh, and it works! A confrontational approach like this one, however, is less likely to be needed if you are using

## If you must urgently criticize someone you do not know well, establish acceptable expectations first

the giver methodology chart as it is designed. But what if there is an urgent need to criticize, and you don't have time to find out the receiver's preference? Your option, then, is to establish some expectations immediately prior to giving the criticism. For example, you might say: "Let's agree to listen carefully to each other before commenting. Do you agree?" If the receiver agrees, you can then raise the second expectation, which addresses the need to agree on when the meeting will end. Again, it's imperative that you wait for the response before proceeding further with the conversation. Too often, we get so wrapped up in anticipation of what we want to say next that we forget to wait for the person to agree.

Make sure you ask for an "active" agreement—one that indicates the person truly believes what he is agreeing to. A person who simply nods or says "yes" for the purpose of allowing the conversation to continue is offering a passive agreement. This passive agreement is weak and cannot be relied on. An active agreement, on the other hand, is an affirmative statement by the receiver: "Yes, I agree to..." So, when working with explosive people it's helpful to ensure that they are actively agreeing with you. Otherwise, you run the risk of having communications break down and tensions build up.

Establishing expectations up front makes it easier for the giver and receiver to get back to the issue at hand when emotions start to run high. Rather than getting personal when the receiver interrupts, all the giver needs to say is "Remember our agreement." If the person refuses to agree to terms from the outset, then you really have a much bigger issue to deal with.

## Situation 3
What do you do when a coworker or friend is brilliant at deflecting the criticism?

Again, knowing your receiver (see Step II of the giver methodology chart) is crucial. But in this case, mental preparation (Step III of the giver methodology chart) can be especially helpful in staying focused on the specific issue to be discussed. During mental preparation, work through the exchange, imagining when and how the person will try to catch you off guard and change the subject. Here's one manager who gets trapped by his "deflecting" employee.

MANAGER: Charlie, I can't understand why you don't turn in your corporate receipts on time. You're a good employee, but this is an area that you let slide. It reflects badly on you.

CHARLIE: You know, I can't believe you set up a formal meeting with me to tell me something so insignificant. I get all the major reports in on time when other employees don't, and this past year I achieved every objective. I don't understand why you are making such a big deal out of this.

MANAGER: I'm not making a big deal out of this ...

CHARLIE [*interrupting*]: Yes, you are. I'll get them in. Anything else?

Had the manager taken the time to anticipate Charlie's response, he might have said something like: "Charlie, whether or not you think I'm making a big deal about turning in corporate receipts is not the topic of our discussion. We can talk about that at another time. Right now we are discussing the fact that you turn them in late. So let's make sure we stick to the agenda."

Obviously, you can't expect to always know what a person will say. But by investing time in mentally rehearsing your criticism, you'll be much more attuned to "deflectors" and therefore in a much better position to bring them back to your agenda. In fact, when you are in the process of actually delivering the criticism, be sure to clarify the agenda and keep it in the forefront of your mind as you listen calmly to what the receiver is saying.

### Situation 4

What do you do when the receiver has agreed with you in the past about the need to change but fails to take any corrective action?

Let's explore this situation from an off-the-job perspective. Susan's tendency to take too much time preparing herself to go out to dinner infuriates her husband, Bill. Typically, he yells at her and Susan agrees that it's inconsiderate. But invariably she does it again.

One day, Bill tries a different approach. He tells Susan's close friend, Carol, that he is frustrated by how much time Susan takes getting ready to go out to dinner. Carol, in turn, speaks to Susan about her conversation with Bill. Susan realizes that she is causing Bill real anguish and then tries her best to resolve the problem. In this case, it takes a third person to drive home the criticism. Although Bill is her husband, Susan's persistent rejection of his criticism, for whatever reason, indicates he isn't the best person to deliver the criticism.

It is not uncommon for managers to find themselves faced with a receiver who agrees about the need to change but takes no action. Like Bill, a manager in this kind of situation might carefully examine what typically happens during the criticism exchange. Does it turn into an "I'm right/you're wrong" match? What needs to happen between giver and receiver so that the focus of the exchange is on appropriate action to take and a review of consequences?

In the case of Bill and Susan, Bill was hard pressed to offer meaningful consequences: He could cancel their dinner reservations if she didn't speed up, but that would hurt him, too.

In a typical manager/employee relationship, however, there would be clear consequences if no action is taken. Talking about consequences forces the receiver to focus on the expected behavior in relation to the criticism and prevents viewing the criticism abstractly or as unfair treatment. During these discussions, it is extremely important to pay attention to the manner and expression of delivery. Keep it matter-of-fact—that way you will avoid sending undesirable messages that could complicate things further.

### Situation 5

What do you do when the person you have to criticize is unwilling to admit errors and instead blames others?

First, consider this. What difference does it make whether the person admits the error? Remember, criticism is delivered for the purpose of getting the person to take some desired action. Whether the receiver admits he is wrong is of secondary importance. More important than concerning yourself with an individual's unwillingness to admit errors is recognizing that a person who continually blames others will be less apt to see any need to take corrective action.

There are three effective approaches for dealing with the person who habitually blames others. The first approach involves establishing a clear expectation that blaming others is unacceptable behavior and will not be tolerated. If the person still lapses into the pattern of blaming others, then all you need to do is refer back to the mutual expectation. There is no need to continue with that particular aspect of the conversation.

Are you cutting the person off? Not exactly. You're simply reminding the person of the mutually-agreed-upon expectation. Receivers will typically respond favorably because rather than personally attacking them, you're simply referring them back to the agreed-upon expectation.

The second approach involves clarifying expectations about taking responsibility for a task. Prior to assigning a task or project, clarify what the individual is responsible for and exactly what that means. When he attempts to blame others, he is not taking responsibility, as agreed. Again, no further discussion is necessary.

If, however, you want to see if there is some legitimacy to what is being said, try the third approach—calling the person on what he is saying. When he accuses specific people of not following through on an assignment, for example, stop the conversation and bring everyone whose name is mentioned into your office. In an open atmosphere, ask each employee exactly what went on. Use this confrontational meeting as an opportune time to clarify what being responsible means and how blaming others is a practice you will not tolerate. Your message will get everyone's attention and will be easily understood.

## Recognize personal preference in critical styles, but always avoid personalizing the message

### Situation 6

What do you do when you have to deliver criticism that may hurt another person's feelings?

This is a particularly challenging situation to address because you have no control over the receiver's feelings. And if the subject of the criticism is particularly sensitive, the receiver may feel hurt.

Hurt is often unavoidable and may itself inspire action. You can, however, minimize the hurt by considering how the receiver prefers being criticized. Even though having to criticize is uncomfortable, there can be good feelings between the giver and receiver because both realize that the receiver's individual criticism preference has not been ignored.

It's also valuable to avoid personalizing your message. In other words, instead of saying, "You did not get this report completed according to specifications," simply say, "This report is not completed according to specifications." You will convey the same message, only the receiver's focus will be more on the criticism than on himself.

### CONCLUSION

This chapter has highlighted some of the more common situations that arise when giving criticism. Obviously, it's impossible to address every circumstance that might occur. As long as you take the time to prepare delivering criticism to an individual, you're not likely to be totally thrown by his response. Being properly prepared means thoroughly answering each of the questions in the giver methodology chart in Chapter 3. For extra help in highly emotional situations, refer to the giver action plan in Appendix C.

## CHAPTER 5

# Responding to Criticism as the Receiver: Using Control Effectively

---

### *Situation*

Tom, vice-president for new product development at a manufacturing company, calls Jerry and Mary, his two direct reports, into his office. Each had been working long hours to complete a project that had very tight deadlines—largely because the company wanted to capture a narrow market window for the new product being introduced.

TOM: Jerry and Mary, I know that managing the development of our new product hasn't been easy. You had numerous design changes that threatened meeting the deadline. I'm glad to say that your teams were successful; however, it wasn't without several costly errors. We simply can't operate without regard to adhering to budget restraints. I had to defend your actions to my boss—and it wasn't easy. I'm counting on both of you to make sure we maintain high quality while keeping costs under control.

JERRY: Tom, like you, Mary and I want to maintain high quality and cost effectiveness. Frankly, we need your help. We could do a better job of checking parts coming in from our suppliers and minimize costs resulting from overtime if we could meet with you regularly each week to handle order changes and needed purchases. What do you think of our meeting more regularly with a focus on budget control?

TOM: Good suggestion. Let me know when it's convenient.

Tom's phone rings and he excuses himself, gesturing for Mary and Jerry to leave. Outside Tom's office Mary commends Jerry for the way he handled what could have been a very explosive meeting.

MARY: I don't know how you did it, Jerry. I almost lost my temper when Tom said he had to defend our actions to his boss. After all, he's a major source of our frustration. Tom is never available and we can't do anything without his approval. You certainly handled that situation tactfully. I wish I could control myself as well as you do.

**Question**

How did Jerry avoid becoming defensive and how did he turn a potentially negative situation into something positive?

■   In this chapter, we will introduce the receiver control chart, a valuable device for learning how to use the control that inherently belongs to the receiver of criticism.

Before exploring how to better use the control that is inherently that of the receiver, let's look at some important insights surrounding criticism.

- Don't be thrown by a giver's manner of delivery—givers think they are right.
- Keep an open mind—one can reject the criticism at any point.
- Words can hurt, but it is essential to look beyond the words at the intent of the criticism.
- The receiver colors what is being said.
- The ability to accept criticism varies, depending on who is delivering the criticism.
- If the giver is attempting to deliver quality criticism, it is the receiver's responsibility to make him or her feel comfortable.
- The giver is just as uncomfortable delivering the criticism as the receiver is in getting it.
- The worst thing to do as the receiver is to react defensively or become argumentative; this kind of behavior precludes any meaningful discussion.
- Receiving criticism is uncomfortable because:
  — The giver is pointing out something negative or is expressing some form of disapproval.

— Criticism implies that you will need to make a change.

Keep these important ideas in mind as you read through each step in the receiver control chart (see pages 56 and 57). The chart is designed to help the receiver keep an open mind, view criticism as merely information, and sort out quality criticism from other more destructive forms of criticism. Rather than feel helpless, the receiver uses the receiver control chart to engage in a dialogue to identify the productive value to be gained from the criticism. Specifically, the receiver is better able to validate the criticism, identify what corrective action needs to be taken, and identify the value to be gained from making an effort to change.

Another purpose of the receiver control chart is to help de-emotionalize the criticism. Keeping emotions in check will better enable one to sort out the intentions behind the criticism and keep it in proper perspective so that one can benefit from what is being communicated. The receiver control chart is divided into three steps. Each step is designed to help the receiver deal with the criticism itself as well as the person delivering the criticism.

Step I of the receiver control chart acknowledges the receiver's natural tendency to question who is communicating the criticism. Step II, on the other hand, focuses the receiver's attention on the criticism itself. The questions in Step II are directed at ensuring that productive value can be gained from the criticism. Step III takes into account the receiver's emotions. Each question helps the receiver examine how he feels about the criticism and whether or not he is willing to take action. With all these steps in mind, let's analyze the process of handling criticism once it is delivered.

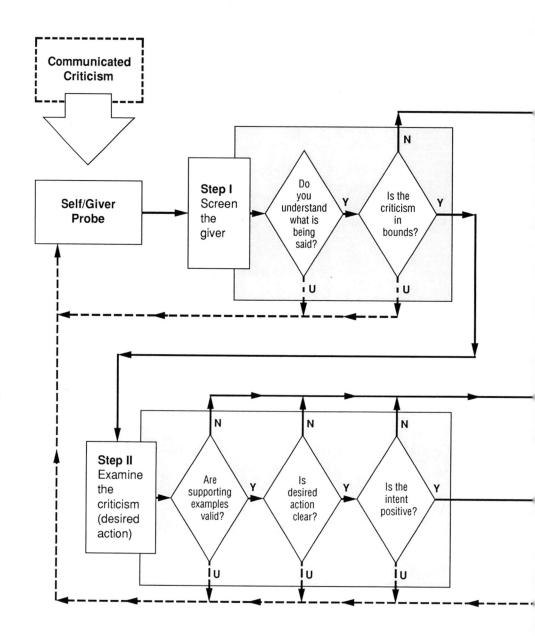

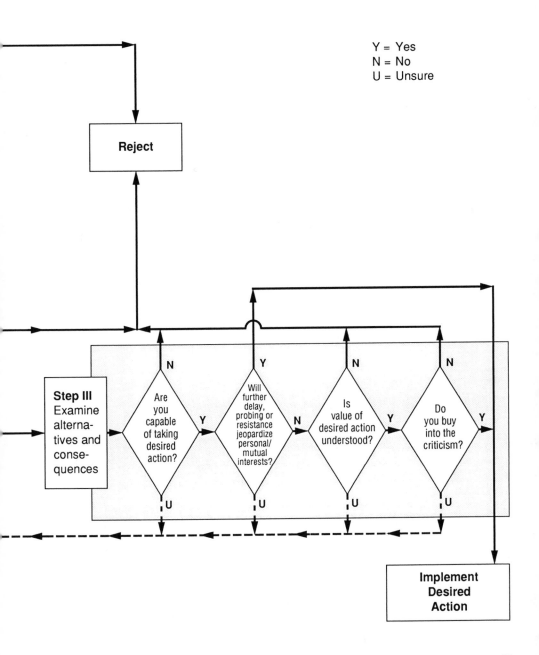

Y = Yes
N = No
U = Unsure

Reject

**Step III**
Examine alternatives and consequences

Are you capable of taking desired action?

Will further delay, probing or resistance jeopardize personal/mutual interests?

Is value of desired action understood?

Do you buy into the criticism?

**Implement Desired Action**

## Focus on *what* is being said, rather than *how* it is communicated

### STEP I: SCREEN THE GIVER

Focusing on *who* is delivering criticism is a natural response and can color what is being said. Keep an open mind as you consider the questions discussed below.

■ ***Do you understand what is being said?***

Understanding what is being said encompasses both hearing and understanding. For example, if the giver yells at the receiver, the receiver may be focusing more on the tone of the criticism than on the content. Likewise, if the giver uses certain emotionally charged words, the receiver may tune out and miss what is really being communicated.

The receiver's willingness to hear what is being said very much depends on his past experiences with the giver and the quality of the relationship. If the receiver has little respect for the giver, chances are great that the criticism will be ignored. Here's a good example: A teacher who has been in the profession for 15 years is criticized for how he prepares lesson plans by a young assistant principal. He says to her, "Who are you to tell me how I should write lesson plans? You have probably written only a few in your entire career!" In this situation, what could have been usable advice got discarded in favor of a kind of pride in seniority. The point was missed and the relationship put in jeopardy.

At the same time that the receiver is attempting to hear what is being said, he is also determining whether it is a criticism and whether the giver is talking in understandable terms.

*Caveat*: Taking control as the receiver means making sure you listen to understand versus listening to judge.

*Caveat*: Taking control as the receiver means that it is important to focus on *what* is being said instead of being overly sensitive to *how* it is being communicated.

### ■ *Is the criticism in bounds?*

This question addresses whether the criticism is within the bounds of the relationship. If your boss were to say to you that you are spending too much time at work and are neglecting loved ones at home, you may reject the criticism: What you do with your personal time is up to you. Similarly, if a peer were to criticize you for the way you handled a customer, you may decide that she had no right to say anything to you because she is not your boss. In both cases, less any rationale as to why they were qualified, it would seem that you would be right in rejecting what was said.

The timing of criticism is also a factor in determining whether it is appropriate. There are days, for example, when everything seems to go wrong. And just when you think the day is over, your boss comes over to you and points out a mistake. At that moment you may admit that you can't handle another thing—the criticism is temporarily rejected because of bad timing. Similarly, when the criticism is delivered in public or is consistently delivered prior to entering an important meeting or event, it's natural to question whether the criticism is meant to help or hinder.

Once the receiver determines that the criticism is within bounds and is willing to listen further, the chart directs the receiver to Step II, where the focus is on validating the criticism and determining whether productive outcomes can result.

## STEP II: EXAMINE THE CRITICISM (DESIRED ACTION)

The receiver of criticism should carefully examine the criticism in order to understand the desired outcome. The questions discussed below help to focus the receiver's examination of the criticism.

■ *Are supporting examples valid?*

If the giver is unable to provide specific examples to support the criticism, the receiver may question the giver's intent. The same holds true if the receiver feels that the examples cited are not valid. Rather than reject the criticism, the receiver may want to probe further. But without any specific examples, the criticism may be too vague to respond to with any kind of corrective action.

Mary did this when a peer of hers, Joe, critiqued a presentation she had given. Some of his criticisms did not match what anyone else had said. So, Mary asked Joe to explain himself further. Joe's response made it clear to Mary that he had not given a lot of thought to his comments, because he cited no specifics. As a result, Mary concluded that his criticism was not valid, and she rejected it. Mary was right to do this because she had no specifics to focus on in order to understand his point.

Besides validating the criticism, the receiver needs to know the corrective action desired. This is addressed by asking:

■ *Is the desired action clear?*

Even if the criticism lacks validity, the suggested action may be a good one. Knowing the specific action to take is one of the most important things to walk away with at the end of the exchange. If the receiver does not have a clear idea of what it is she needs to do and is left guessing, more criticism may result.

Let's say, for example, that a boss tells an employee that he "needs to improve his attitude." On one level this is good information, but on another level the insight is meaningless. The employee needs to ask for specifics and reassurance that when put into practice, the specific actions would demonstrate a better attitude. If the boss is unwilling to provide the necessary specifics, then the employee may rightfully question the intent of the criticism. Two key points to keep in mind: (1) Knowing the specific action desired means knowing what the giver *perceives* as the desired action required and (2) receivers may subject themselves to more criticism when they take action on what *they* perceive is the desired action when it is, in fact, not the desired action.

*Caveat:* Taking control as the receiver means that if you typically get defensive when criticism is delivered, you may find it helpful to say nothing. When you've had a chance to think about it, go back to the giver and discuss appropriate actions to take. Again, as is always true, the mind should rule over emotions.

Deciding to accept and take corrective action on the criticism is dependent upon the receiver's concern about the giver's intentions. To help clarify this important concern, ask:

■ ### Is the intent positive?

Being able to sort out the intentions behind the criticism is a valuable way for the receiver to exercise control. Here's an example: Just as you walk through the door, your mate says, "I can't believe you are so late, we have nothing to eat and

I'm starved! And I bet you forgot to pick up my clothes from the cleaners." (Notice that you haven't said anything yet, not even "hello.") After examining what your mate is saying and questioning his intention, you will probably conclude that he's had a bad day and his only intent is to take it out on you. So if the receiver is unsure of the giver's intention, she should ask directly: "What is your purpose?" In this case, the intent was not positive. In other cases, the intent may be positive, but the receiver does not perceive it as such because he or she is focusing more on how it is being communicated than on what is being said.

Discussions with hundreds of people during workshops have revealed clues to look for when trying to determine the intent behind criticism. The following are some of the more common clues for the receiver to look for on the part of the giver of criticism. These clues should send an immediate signal to the receiver that the giver's intent may not be positive.

- Approaches you knowing that it will upset you
- Talks in generalities
- Fails to look you in the eye
- Is quick to cut you off
- Exaggerates the criticism
- Offers no corrective action
- Compares you to an identified known enemy

If one or more of these clues are present, then the receiver might want to ask for clarification of the giver's intention. A good question to ask to clarify the intent behind the criticism is: "How do you want me to take this?" or "How should I take this?" Tone of voice plays a big part in the giver's response.

If the receiver's goal is to add fuel to the conversation, the question should be asked in a challenging tone of voice. If the receiver's intention is to truly understand where the giver is coming from, then the question should be asked in a questioning tone of voice that seeks to understand and not to condemn. If the receiver is not satisfied that the intent of the giver is really to help, *the criticism should be rejected.* For whatever reason, sometimes the receiver says the right thing at the wrong time or mishandles the criticism. Emotions seem to win over logic and the receiver's ability to be sensitive to what really is going on gets lost.

Step III from the chart helps the receiver manage emotions and sort out what is happening in the larger picture.

## STEP III: EXAMINE ALTERNATIVES AND CONSEQUENCES

There may be times when questioning the criticism puts the receiver in the familiar position of "winning the battle but losing the war." For instance, if your mate is explosively venting outlandish criticisms on you, it might be best to nod your head and simply move on. Even a reasonable question probing for intent or more specifics might do little more than start World War III.

In other words, it is helpful to consider the circumstances surrounding the criticism, which includes assessing emotional levels. By doing this, the receiver automatically captures a global view of the issue. Viewing the situation in a macro perspective helps the receiver determine how best to respond. As past experience with certain givers has demonstrated, sometimes it's best to simply accept what is being communicated at the moment rather than trying to engage in a dialogue.

The ability to accurately interpret the situation as it is unfolding becomes intuitive after a while. There are some key questions, which we will now explore, to help receivers sharpen their focus and their sensitivity to the situation.

### ■ *Are you capable of taking desired action?*

Regardless of the fact that one is convinced that the criticism is clear, in bounds, based on specifics, and has a positive intent behind it, it may be impossible to proceed toward desired action simply because the receiver is not properly equipped to take action.

For example, a recently hired administrative assistant at a fast-paced publicity agency was criticized by his boss for repeatedly failing to correctly proof grammatical mistakes in a number of press releases. While the boss approached the new employee with prepared sensitivity and clearly pointed out the oversights with an eye toward helping the new hire, the new administrative assistant became frustrated in a very short time and had to sort out his feelings and admit that grammar and punctuation were not among his strengths. He was the wrong person for the job—it was that simple.

When faced with an inability to move toward corrective action, the receiver must admit this lack of ability in order to avoid the perception that the criticism is being rejected by nature of no action—a condition that could only worsen the predicament.

■ ***Will further delay, probing, or resistance
jeopardize personal/mutual interests?***

All phases of the receiver control chart are important and all
require a certain degree of astuteness on the part of the
receiver. While all the judgments are qualified ones, none
demands quite as much intuitiveness as deciding what really
is at stake if action on the criticism is delayed beyond what
the giver considers reasonable, or if asking too many questions or resisting action is attempted. In making this judgment, the receiver must rely on all that is known about the
giver—the spoken and unspoken expectations, the intensity
of the giver's delivery, and observations made of like situations as they occurred when others were involved with the
giver. Whatever it takes, the judgment should be made
quickly, and if the answer to this question is "yes," the
receiver should move on to implementing the desired action
immediately, unless the receiver decides that risking the
relationship is more desirable.

If after rapid but careful reflection the receiver is unsure
whether further delay, probing, or resistance might place his
position or the relationship in jeopardy, then one well-cal-
culated probing question is the best alternative: "Is this of
immediate importance to you or could I have time to consider my reaction?" If given time, the receiver moves on to
the next question.

■ ***Is the value of desired action understood?***

This is an important question. Adults are not inclined to do
things just because they are told to. They may appear to be
doing what was asked but really are just going through the
motions. Letting the receiver know the value of the desired

action will ensure that the receiver will make a genuine effort in taking action on the criticism.

As the receiver, if you are unsure about the value to be gained by taking action on the criticism, probe further by asking the giver for more specifics, or allow for some personal time to sort things out. There's no reason why the receiver can't go back to the giver several days later and further explore the potential value of the criticism.

*Caveat:* If the criticism has no value, the receiver may reject it.

If the value associated with the criticism is understood, then the receiver moves to the next question in the receiver control chart. There the receiver will have a chance to reconsider what is being asked of him as the final assessment of whether to buy into the criticism is made.

### ■ *Do you buy into the criticism?*

Considering whether you, as the receiver, buy into the criticism is your opportunity to determine if you have an understanding of what specifically you are to do to correct the situation. If you don't know what specific actions to take, you cannot buy into the criticism. But rather than reject it, try probing further.

Determining if you buy into the criticism also gives you a chance to reflect on whether you focused more on how the criticism was being delivered than on what was being said. Re-examining the giver's intentions, when and where the criticism was delivered, and if the criticism is credible are the kinds of questions the receiver should explore before finally accepting the criticism.

Time is also an important factor in determining whether you buy into the criticism. Sometimes, it's best to heed advice you may have heard from your parents or other significant people: "Things will be better in the morning." If you are tired or upset, or if you don't trust the giver, you may need some time to let things settle.

*Caveat:* Remember, you are in control—this means you do not need to respond immediately.

Your emotions play an important part in determining whether you buy into the criticism. Each of us has developed a "typical" response to criticism. Some of us respond to the initial criticism more emotionally than others. If this is your typical response, then perhaps it's advisable to let time work for you before deciding whether you accept the criticism and are willing to take action. By the same token, if you're the kind of person who has built a wall of resistance against criticism, you may need to chip away at the wall and come to the realization that criticism does have value.

## CONCLUSION

Dealing effectively with criticism, especially if it is of a sensitive nature, can be difficult. The degree of difficulty may vary from one day to the next, but the receiver who follows each step in the chart will be in a much better position to accept the criticism and act on it, or, if appropriate, reject it. The following receiver checklist helps to focus the receiver in trying to understand the criticism and outlines the discussion of the receiver control chart given in this chapter.

## RECEIVER CHECKLIST

As the receiver of criticism, ask yourself the following questions:

1. Do you understand what is being said?
2. Will you accept criticism from this person?
3. Is the criticism in bounds?
4. Are the supporting examples valid?
5. Do you understand the desired action?
6. Is the intent of the criticism positive?
7. Are you capable of taking the desired action?
8. Will delaying or probing further jeopardize personal interests?
9. Does the criticism fit in with mutual and individual goals?
10. Is the value of the desired action understood?
11. Do you buy into the criticism?

If the answer to every question on the checklist is "yes," move on to the next step—take action. If the answer to any question is "no," reject the criticism. If you are unsure of any of the answers, ask more questions of yourself and the giver.

# Overcoming Common Difficulties When Receiving Criticism: What Do You Say, and When?

### Situation

It's 7:00 p.m., and Jane has just returned home from work. Normally, she's home by 6:00 p.m., but this day Jane's supervisor was home with the flu and Jane had to oversee several meetings and prepare a report, which was sent by messenger to her supervisor's home. Jane's husband, Bill, greets her at the door and the following conversation takes place.

BILL: Hi, sweetheart. Had a long day, didn't you? By the way, did you get in touch with the electrician today?

JANE: No, Bill. I tried but...

BILL: What do you mean, no! I thought we agreed last night that it was important to talk with them today. I can't believe you!

JANE: Bill, I...

BILL: I can never count on you to follow through on anything. You get too wrapped up in your work. All it would have taken was a simple phone call. I guess I have to take care of everything myself. I should have...

### Question

What can a receiver say or do when the criticism seems to come out of left field and is poorly delivered?

■ It would be wishful thinking to expect all givers of criticism to prepare themselves properly by following the giver methodology chart (see Chapter 3). But more often than not givers lack eloquence in delivering criticism.

This chapter will equip you to be even better at receiving criticism, especially when it is delivered by unskilled givers. Surveys conducted in conjunction with workshops on the power of positive criticism show that unskilled givers seem to fall into various patterns. Maybe you've recently had an encounter with a giver who:

- Strings 'em together
- Hits and runs
- Exaggerates the criticism
- Publicly criticizes
- Criticizes you for doing what you were told

Let's explore some situations in which these various giver patterns surface and at the same time introduce some proven responses for better handling them.

## Situation 1

What do you say when you are presented with a string of criticisms?

Here's an example. Sharon is a claims processor for an insurance company based on the West Coast. One day, after returning from a coffee break, Sharon finds an urgent note from Mindy, her boss, asking her to come by immediately.

"Sharon," Mindy begins as soon as Sharon opens the office door, "these claims you left for me are a mess! I can't make heads or tails of them. And while we're on the subject of messes, you might think about organizing your desk. You have paper piled on paper—it's a wonder you can find anything! And one more thing—your coffee breaks have been too long. You know the rules around here. Why not follow them?"

Sharon could say: "You conveyed a lot of information, Mindy. Could I have some time with you to go over these problems?"

## The value of criticism can be lost if many issues are strung together

Without automatically rejecting the criticism, Sharon is helping Mindy see that while the criticism may have value, the value gets lost when too many issues are strung together.

There are other approaches to take when faced with a "string 'em together" criticizer. One approach is to refrain from saying anything at all—especially when the giver comes across as very upset—and simply nod your head (and possibly give a smile). This acknowledges that you're listening to the criticism. Nothing more, nothing less. Use your good judgment in determining whether silence momentarily might be the best tactic.

Sometimes, a particularly valuable approach is to ask, "What's your purpose?" Asking this helps the giver put the criticism in proper perspective and sort out the intent behind it. At the same time, the receiver who asks this question slows down the momentum and demonstrates skillfulness in probing the giver. This particular question qualifies as a "quick charge." Remember, a quick charge is a technique that can be used on the spot to help receivers maintain self-control and thus better handle a situation. Quick charges are indispensable tools, and are all the more valuable because no one can detect when they are being used. Asking "What's your purpose?" successfully often depends on using a questioning tone of voice that conveys the idea of genuinely wanting to get more information. (More quick changes will be introduced later in this chapter.)

## Situation 2

What do you say when the giver hits and runs?

> Alice is riding in the elevator with her boss, Susan. They're on their way to a meeting with upper management to discuss preliminary design plans for a proposal to a potential client. Susan breaks the silence by criticizing Alice for wearing too much make-up.
>
> Alice responds defensively: "Who are you to tell me I'm wearing too much make-up?"
>
> The elevator door opens and the conversation comes to an abrupt end. With the "hit and run" criticizer, there is no time to respond or enter into probing dialogues. In situations like these, receivers need to focus on the intent of what is being said and determine whether, as is most often the case, the giver is attempting to hurt or disarm the receiver, rather than trying to help. Whatever might be the case, if you are the receiver of a "hit and run" criticism, don't let it get to you. Instead, file it for a future and more appropriate time and place where you can discuss the intent with the giver.

## Situation 3

What do you say when the criticism is exaggerated?

> There will be times in your career when you encounter the criticizer who exaggerates everything—especially mistakes. For example: "I can't believe this report is such a wreck. If I were to present this report in front of my peers and my boss, I'd be the laughingstock of the division. You're supposed to be my right-hand person—how could you turn in such an awful report and have the nerve to tell me it's complete?" When the criticism explodes in your face, it's essential to

inspect what is really being said and who is saying it. It's too early to reject the criticism. Your more immediate concern is to try to uncover some specifics. Take the time to view the giver objectively and examine what's behind the criticism.

Chances are great that givers who exaggerate do so frequently. Having this insight makes it easier to accept the situation and focus on what's really being said instead of taking a defensive posture. While defensiveness might be a natural response to being "blasted," it doesn't permit the receiver to focus on the criticism for what it is. In the example above, perhaps what is behind the criticism and what is making the boss so upset is the receiver's lack of attention to detail and concern for quality work. Therefore, when faced with the giver who exaggerates criticism, sort out what is really being said and listen to understand, not to judge. Instinct may tell the receiver that the best response is to say nothing at all and to simply wait for an appropriate time to question for specifics. At a later time, when emotions have cooled down, the giver may be more approachable for clarifying specifics.

Another response might be: "I can understand your being upset. I, too, dislike it when work comes in and it's of a poor quality. It looks as if people don't take pride in what they do. But I do. Can you tell me exactly what it is you don't like?"

Agreeing with the giver takes the edge off the criticism and skillfully gets the giver to frame the criticism in specific terms and start discussing corrective action.

In order to help remain calm, it's useful to practice the breathing quick charge. This quick charge will keep your emotions in check, while at the same time enable you to think more clearly. These benefits are possible because when encountering tense situations, your body will naturally operate in a contrary manner. In other words, your brain needs an ample supply of oxygen in order to function effectively. However, when you get uptight your breathing will become short and choppy—thus depriving the brain of the very oxygen it needs.

To practice the breathing quick charge, inhale slowly and smoothly through your nose, hold momentarily, and then exhale once again through your nostrils, allowing the air to escape slowly. At the same time you're exhaling, relax all of your muscles, preferably starting at your head and progressing down to your feet. The real pay-off is in the smooth exhalation, in combination with the relaxation of your muscles. Keep in mind that you are learning to capitalize on the familiar "sigh" and using it to a much greater advantage!

## Situation 4

What do you say when public criticism strikes?

A newly appointed supervisor, Jim, experiences the horror of public criticism at a staff meeting when Bernice, his boss, blasts him for delays in his department. "Your department is an embarrassment to everyone working on this project. You're the supervisor—you're supposed to oversee the work that's being done. It's my bet that you're spending too much time at your desk." Jim could try to defend himself. Or he could instantly implement the "Excuse me?" quick charge. This quick charge is practiced by simply saying "excuse me" with a questioning tone of voice. With the proper inflection, this is a good, indirect way to get the giver to repeat herself. In the process of repeating herself, the giver is likely to realize what she has done and will instantly decide to drop the discussion.

While the "Excuse me?" quick charge will typically catch the giver off-guard (and possibly embarrass her), it won't necessarily prevent public criticism in the future. So this approach needs to be used with caution.

The best approach for dealing with public criticism is to privately talk to the giver some time after the criticism has been delivered. If you find yourself talking to a brick wall, and the issue becomes bothersome, it may be necessary to take greater risks—go to human resources, or escalate the issue to a higher level of management. If all else fails, you may need to take desparate steps to change your job.

### Situation 5
What do you say when you are criticized for doing what you were told to do?

Here's an awkward situation. Terry is told to pull together information from certain files for a monthly report his boss is preparing. When he delivers the material for his boss to review, he is caught by surprise. "This isn't what I need," his boss says. Terry could instantly reply: "It's what you asked me to get." That's a perfectly legitimate response that many people in his situation would opt for. However, an important underlying issue is: Do you criticize your boss in responding to what you perceive as unfair criticism?

Obviously, the answer depends a lot on your relationship with your boss and the present environment. A word of advice: If you are unsure, it's best not to criticize your boss. The risk is too great that you may win the battle but lose the war!

If the relationship you have with your boss is strong and built on mutual respect, then you might say, "You know, I don't mind admitting I'm wrong and accepting responsibility for my errors, but in this case—believe it or not—I thought I was doing what you asked me to do." Then turn your focus to what needs to be done in the event you were wrong.

Using humor in this situation can also be effective. But whatever tactic you choose, be sensitive to the circumstances surrounding the criticism and be aware of unspoken expectations. For example, if you sense your boss has had a rough day, it may be best to simply say nothing and do what's necessary to correct things. You might want to correct the record later—like over lunch or at an informal meeting after work.

Again, it is best to avoid being defensive. If it happens often, make it a practice to summarize in writing tasks as they are delegated. That way, you'll eliminate the possibility of future confrontations caused by misunderstandings.

## CONCLUSION

Using control as the receiver means learning how to better respond to criticism that is delivered by unskilled givers. Rather than getting caught off-guard, throughout this chapter receivers have learned that through the use of quick charges and by relying on the receiver control chart (see Chapter 5), potentially explosive situations can be warded off and thus handled more effectively.

Receivers have also learned that sometimes the best thing to do is to say nothing and simply take action.

Little has been said about using humor—that's not to imply that it's not valuable. Humor is a great way to rebound from criticisms that catch you off-guard. You just need to be masterful when using it. It can backfire.

This leads to the importance of relying upon your own instincts and prior experiences. After all, personalities will differ, as do circumstances. So, there are no absolute answers.

The insights presented throughout this chapter are to help you better use the control that is inherently yours when you are the receiver of criticism—by understanding this you'll feel empowered.

To help you put the quick charges discussed in this chapter into practice, a quick summary is provided. Remember, quick charges are techniques that can be used on-the-spot to help receivers maintain self control and thus better handle stressful situations. Another advantage to using quick charges is that no one can detect when they are being implemented.

- *"What's your purpose?" quick charge.*

  This quick charge helps the giver put the criticism in the proper perspective and sort out the intent behind it. It is an effective way to probe the giver without causing a defensive reaction. Using a questioning tone of voice helps to ensure the successful implementation of this quick charge.

- *Breathing quick charge.*

  This quick charge helps to keep your emotions in check and enables you to think more clearly. Besides helping you to remain in control when receiving criticism, it is valuable to use just prior to making a presentation.

## Quick charges help receivers maintain control to handle stressful situations better

Remember, the real pay-off when using this technique is in the smooth exhalation, in combination with the relaxation of all of your muscles.

- *"Excuse me?" quick charge.*

  This quick charge is helpful when encountering intimidating situations, like when a giver blasts you with a chain of criticisms. By simply saying "excuse me" in a questioning tone of voice, you get the giver to repeat herself. In the process of reciting back what was said, the giver quickly becomes aware of what she has done and will instantly drop the discussion. This quick charge is useful in other intimidating situations when another person is trying to embarrass you, whether during a meeting or a presentation.

Several other quick charges are introduced in this book. They are the wastepaper basket and audio cassette tape quick charges in Chapter 2, and the "so what" quick charge in Chapter 8.

## CHAPTER 7

# Quality Criticism: A Subtle Ingredient of Well-Functioning Teams

## *Situation*

Tom is project leader of an interdepartmental group building a new engine. He is winding up a meeting with Peter and Jerry after getting a rundown of what their departments had been doing.

TOM: Well, this concludes the major topics I wanted to discuss. Is there anything else?

PETER: Yes, I'd like to get an update on the modular system. Jerry, where are we to date on the accelerator pipes?

JERRY: I'm not really prepared to talk about this now. If I'm not mistaken, we have a project review meeting scheduled for next Monday. At our last update meeting, I announced that we had 23 cylinders in place.

PETER: Did you say 23 cylinders completed? What's wrong with you and your group? You should have been at 30.

JERRY: Peter, I'm not sure what you're talking about. Our department is current. We are meeting projected target dates.

PETER: Did you not read the note I sent you two weeks ago asking for five more cylinders to be built immediately?

JERRY: What note are you talking about? If I had known about it, I would have put some people on it right away.

PETER: I included it in the last memorandum I sent you—guess you didn't read it carefully?

JERRY: The 8-page one…

[The room gets a little icy and still.]

PETER: Well, Jerry, you told me you hated reading long reports. I guess this proves that you hate to read memos, too!

Everyone laughs heartily except Jerry. Peter and Jerry return to their offices. Peter gets right down to work while Jerry sits at his desk simmering.

### Question

How does criticism exchange, like the one that took place between Peter and Jerry, affect teamwork?

### Answer

Tremendously! In a team atmosphere, leaders and managers must be ever mindful of the quality of communication between team members and be ready and able to manage that quality. To disregard how members interact and communicate both positive and negative feelings toward one another is to court not only a breakdown of team cooperation, but a catastrophic failure of mission.

■  In the example above, Jerry and Peter were well into beginning a rivalry that could eventually threaten the goal toward which they were working. Who was right and who was wrong is much less important than the way they approached their criticisms. By nature of his passivity, it is Tom who is really most at fault for not directing the quality of the communication between Peter and Jerry. All of them, however, need a lesson in quality criticism.

The subject of teamwork is a familiar one. Most often, whenever a task is too large to be completed by an individual, a team is formed. In order for the team to be a well-functioning team, there has to be trust, respect, and honesty. But what does this have to do with criticism?

Just as quality criticism can serve as a device to motivate an individual within an organization, it can help keep a team functioning at a high level. The improper use of criticism, on the other hand, will chip away at the building blocks of good teamwork. To help understand the subtle effects criticism can have on teamwork, let's take a snapshot look at three different organizations.

### Organization 1

A division of a major East Coast organization is working on an important technological development that will impact the industry at large. Time and budgetary considerations are tight. As a result, employees are under intense pressure to perform. Teams are operating lean and mean.

Historically, the organization has had the reputation of being extremely competitive internally. Consequently, when a project team falls behind, members tend to hedge on the status of the project and give the impression that things are fine. They may even go so far as to give inaccurate information even when knowing full well that the work of other teams will be affected.

Because of the internal competitiveness that exists, upper management doesn't hear about a problem until it has escalated into a big problem for which no one department or individual can take responsibility and be criticized. As a result, everyone takes the heat. In the meantime, the organization suffers because precious management time has been wasted trying to uncover the source of the problem—which is never completely disclosed. At the core of these seemingly complicated variables can be found an essential missing ingredient—the ability to give and receive criticism without endangering team conviviality.

### Organization 2

A medium-sized organization located in the South is working on a major government contract. Individuals with particularly high levels of expertise in aeronautics from all over the world have been asked to work on the project.

As soon as the group begins its work, serious problems arise. At the root of some of the problems is the unacknowledged tension between the design team and the researchers. Although on the surface everyone seems to be working as a team, there is in fact a great deal of backbiting between the groups, which becomes acute during project review meetings. They frequently turn into sharp debates in which harsh words are exchanged. At a recent meeting, a world-renowned researcher criticized one of the engineers for not keeping up with deadlines and accused him of jeopardizing the successful completion of the project. After the meeting, the engineer refused to talk or work with the researcher.

Criticism, rather than being absent from the communication process, is in this case all too obviously used to diminish productivity, not assist it.

### Organization 3

A medium-sized electronics company located in the Midwest has managed to maintain a spirit of family among employees while continuing to grow. Everyone is willing to help each other out and people care about one another. The problem within the "family," however, is that no one wants to confront (i.e., criticize) anyone for fear of hurting feelings and marring the atmosphere. Consequently, certain employees seem to take on greater responsibilities than others and bad feelings linger, dampening motivational levels. Most disturbing to the president is that work quality is inconsistent and due dates are frequently missed.

## GUIDELINES FOR MANAGING QUALITY CRITICISM IN THE TEAM ENVIRONMENT

As the above examples show, the mishandling of criticism breeds dishonesty, break downs in relationships, interference with the free flow of ideas and information, and the construction of walls between people and departments.

Just as praise is a well-known necessity in motivating others, so too is criticism necessary to the creation of an environment built on trust, respect, and honesty. To have teams that function well, managers need to

1. *Make criticism part of a routine day.*

   Address "criticism" up-front in a matter-of-fact way. Help employees understand that to criticize is as integral a part of doing business as paying bills. In order for a group to be a well-functioning team, it must operate with a level of honesty that necessitates leaving room for criticism.

2. *Let the leader's role be known.*

   While it seems that the role of a leader is obvious, too often the leader's expectations are unclear. In order to keep everyone focused and to minimize the misuse of precious energy, it is helpful to establish mutual expectations among leaders and team members for the purpose of clarifying whether the leader is to arbitrate disagreements, handle disputes, and ensure the active participation of all team members.

3. *Promote the idea that results are mutually shared.*

   To avoid witchhunts, help team members understand that everyone is responsible for the outcome of a project: Either it gets successfully completed or it falters. Team members need to take responsibility for checking if some aspect of a project is falling behind and to chip in to see that the deadline can be successfully met. It may mean allocating additional people, resources, time, or money. The focus is on doing whatever it takes to complete the project. Emphasize the use of "we" more than "I." Both criticism and praise need to be conveyed in a way that is consistent with well-functioning team messages. For instance, when a manager praises an individual for her work on a project and neglects to mention important contributions by others, team members may feel slighted. After all, they worked *as a team*, and everyone expects to share the glory.

4. *Establish and enforce team rules of etiquette.*

   Team leaders are well-advised to create operating "credos," or a kind of team constitution. For example:

   - *Avoid public name calling.* It is off-limits to publicly call other team members stupid, dumb, etc.
   - *Refrain from backing someone into a corner.* This means exactly what it says. Too often, team players try to single out a member and publicly knock them around—perhaps in an effort to look good in front of higher management.
   - *Avoid surprises.* Once the agenda has been set and the issues identified, team members are out of bounds if they bring up foreign issues. Avoiding surprises also means making sure that all pertinent information that might bear on the project's overall success is communicated effectively and in a timely manner. This rule, therefore, implies that it's off-limits to play the game, "If the right question is asked, then the one asking will get the right answer."

- *Find opportunities to share glory.* For some reason, team members want to hold all the credit. This team rule says voluntarily look for opportunities to praise or reward others. When something was done successfully in your area, but was dependent upon the input from another department, it's valuable to publicly acknowledge by name the other department's contribution—and meetings are a great place to do this.
- *Do not shoot the bearer of bad news.* When team members "shoot" the bearer of bad news not only are they delivering unfair criticism, they are also promoting an atmosphere that discourages openness and honesty. Rather than focusing on the bad news and what it may mean, this team rule says: Be glad the information is being communicated.
- *Focus on solutions.* Throwing out what's wrong and criticizing events as they unfold is off-limits. This team rule promotes the idea that to criticize is easy. Well-performing team members need to supply solutions or reasonable courses of action to take to rectify a problem or perhaps prevent a similar situation from arising again.

5. *Take the lead to create an atmosphere of openness.*
   The level of honesty within an organization depends a lot on the consistency between the message from its leaders and the actions that follow. To create an atmosphere of openness, these things need to be considered:
   - *More frequent performance reviews.* An organization that conducts only an annual performance review does not send as strong a message that openness is desired as the company that conducts periodic "developmental reviews." The developmental review is a

nonthreatening meeting where the manager reviews the employee's performance. The purpose is to let the employee gain insights on ways to improve performance.

Proponents of this practice say that employees listen better and are more receptive to hearing about issues involving their day-to-day performance because salary increases are not discussed, as they would be during a formal annual review.

- *More open and frequent feedback to employees and peers.* Too often, managers overlook the value to be gained by talking more openly and honestly with employees on an everyday basis and in a casual manner. This means not waiting for a formal performance review to criticize (or praise) an employee's work.
- *Greater willingness to admit mistakes.* A manager who is willing to admit mistakes will greatly influence how others within the group handle and recover from errors and problematic situations. By admitting to a mistake, a manager/team leader conveys a clear message that it's human to err. The important thing, especially in a fiercely competitive environment, is to acknowledge the error quickly after it has occurred so that no time is lost correcting it. When team members see a team leader rebound after an error has been made, it sets a good example for their own behavior and lays the groundwork for an atmosphere of openness within the team.

*Criticism must be managed carefully because it can chip away at promoting teamwork*

## CONCLUSION

Building a climate in which teams perform well is dependent on the consistent usage of the above ingredients. Criticism is an important underlying element, and as subtle as it is in promoting teamwork, it cannot be overlooked. When team members accept criticism as part of the daily routine and focus on finding solutions to problems instead of looking for someone to blame, they are creating an atmosphere where trust, honesty, and respect can thrive.

## CHAPTER 8

# A Word on Self-Criticism

### *Situation*

Carrie Jaynes and Phil Williams are young, aspiring, career-oriented newlyweds working for different organizations. By coincidence, for the past two weeks they have been devoting almost all of their time preparing major presentations to their respective clients. Having made their presentations on the exact same day, they met for dinner to compare the outcomes:

CARRIE: I can't believe I blew it! I worked so hard preparing for that presentation. How could I be so stupid and forget to point out one of the most important features of our new product? You really are dumb, Carrie. My brother was right—I'm just not cut out for the business world. I never thought I would amount to anything, and I was right. I'll never give another presentation. Boy, wait till my boss hears about this. I hope you did well; we might have to rely on your income.

PHIL: I blew it, too! I put so much time into this presentation. How could I have blown it the way I did? I usually give strong presentations. How could I forget to allow time for questions? I can't let that happen again. I've got it! I'll ask someone in the audience to flash a time card informing me of how much time I have left. That should help. Maybe to encourage questions, I could solicit some questions from certain people prior to the presentation. I am just so angry with myself. What can I do to turn these clients around? How can I get them excited about the product? I know, I'll call Charlie tomorrow to work out a recovery strategy.

Both Carrie and Phil are clearly disappointed in themselves. While Phil ends his exercise in self-criticism feeling empowered and challenged to act, Carrie ends up feeling defeated, perhaps paralyzed.

What made the difference in their response and how can self-criticism be managed so that it leads to greater self-confidence? These questions and others are explored in this chapter.

## WHAT IS SELF-CRITICISM?

Self-criticism is a unique aspect of criticism in that the individual engages in a dialogue both as giver and receiver. Almost anything can spark this internal dialogue and no words, it seems, are too harsh. As giver, you know everything there is to know about the receiver and can really pack a punch—until you catch yourself and stop to think: "If you had a friend who talked to you the way you talk to yourself, would you keep him as your friend?" Probably not.

Here's another question that sheds some light on self-criticism: "Do you tolerate mistakes made by others?" Chances are great that you would say "yes." However, if you were to make those same mistakes, would you be as tolerant and forgiving? Probably not.

Why the double standard? Because it's a very human tendency to be harder on ourselves than we are on others. In addition, few of us have taken the time to learn how to turn self-criticism into an asset. So let's take the time to gain a better understanding of self-criticism.

Understanding self-criticism involves recognizing that it is different from self-evaluation. With self-evaluation, an individual objectively assesses herself. It includes both the positive and the negative. Self-criticism is the negative part of self-evaluation and, as has been emphasized throughout this manual, that negativity is what spurs us into action.

There are two types of self-criticism: Real-time self-criticism and longstanding bits of self-criticism. Real-time self-criticism occurs before, during, and after events. Longstanding bits of self-criticism, on the other hand, tend to surface without a specific impetus and are like tape recordings of inner thoughts that have been with the individual for quite some time. Here are some examples of longstanding bits of self-criticism: "I'm so uncoordinated, why attempt anything?" "I'm not good in math." "I'm too laid back." "I'm ugly." No one is without their own redundant tape recording!

Let's return to Carrie and Phil.

Carrie handled her disappointment in a self-destructive way. She took a self-bashing approach, supported by some longstanding bits of self-criticism. The approach used by Phil, on the other hand, is the approach of choice and should be encouraged. Feelings of disappointment and frustration are acknowledged with real-time criticism; at the same time, he redirected the negative by stepping back and examining objectively what he did and what he could do to rectify the situation. As a result, Phil was able to discover ways to improve himself, and that's exciting and motivating! Contributing to the motivation is the belief that it's okay to make mistakes once! The idea is to learn from mistakes so you will keep them from happening a second time.

## In self-criticism, the individual assumes the roles of both giver and receiver

### Forms of Self-Criticism

In order to make optimal use of self-criticism and manage it effectively, we need to become aware of the various forms it takes. Some forms may result in less-than-desirable outcomes, whereas others may create a spark that leads to taking positive action. Consider whether you use some of the following forms of self-criticism.

1. *Public self-criticism.*

   The public self-criticizer is the one who says things like: "I'm always so slow to catch on—would you mind repeating what you just said?" "Gosh, I must be stupid—I don't understand what you are talking about." "I know this is a dumb question, but..."

2. *Fatigued self-criticism.*

   Spontaneous, unsolicited self-criticism is frequently related to fatigue. The negative thoughts may flow late at night or just after a long, hard day at work. One woman in a workshop on criticism demonstrated how fatigue makes her focus on the negative. "I'll walk down the street mentally beating myself up for not being productive and for putting off certain things. In the middle of self-criticism I might remember some important things I accomplished. But negative thoughts overshadow the positive." Regardless of when the negative thoughts arise, be aware if they typically occur when you are tired.

3. *Hindsight self-criticism.*

   Jerry, who owns several restaurants, complains about all the money he would now have if he hadn't managed certain things so poorly. Susan kicks herself repeatedly because the particular project she chose to work on turned out to be a disaster. Tom engages in a boxing match with himself for investing a lot of money in a new business venture that failed. He's beating himself up for losing the money, but the toughest punches are thrown for not being able to see problems ahead of time. In each instance, the criticism would not be possible without hindsight, but the criticizer is angry about not having foresight.

Sometimes sparks fly because we failed to act when the timing was right. The consequences of our actions (or failure to act) are not yet clear, but the criticism still swells. The "I should have" self-criticizer yells at herself for not buying the one-of-a-kind dress at the clothing store or beats himself up for having said something that may have offended a potential client (remember, he doesn't know for sure if he offended the person).

4. *Pre-event self-criticism.*

The pre-event criticizer is the flip side of the hindsight criticizer. The event has not occurred but already the criticisms are taking off. The golfer who stands up to hit the ball and instantly clutters his mind with all kinds of negative thoughts is a classic pre-event criticizer, as is any athlete engaging in a competitive sport. Or it's the executive who takes hours to prepare for an important presentation, all the time feeling anxious and criticizing herself for all the things that may go wrong.

5. *On-the-spot self-criticism.*

The on-the-spot self-criticizer is the salesperson who loses his self-confidence in front of the client because he's mentally telling himself that he's blowing the whole deal. Or it's the engineer who allows the self-criticism to crowd his thoughts during a technical debate so that he finds it difficult to think conceptually.

All of these forms of self-criticism are typically a combination of real-time and longstanding bits of self-criticism. Some parts of them have improvement value while other aspects are simply exercises in self-derogating success blockers.

Hindsight self-criticism most often has the potential of offering a learning point that, when clearly understood, can be of great value in preventing a reoccurrence. One would be wise to try to rid oneself of all the other forms.

## PROCRASTINATION

Procrastination oddly enough can be linked to self-criticism. Each reminder of the need to get something done implies an element of negativity—after all, the procrastinator continues to put off something until the heat is on. Surely many of us have said to ourselves "I'm terrible for not getting to that yet."

People who rely on this approach commonly learned it during school days when they crammed all night to prepare a report or study for an exam. You can easily spot practitioners of this approach in the workplace: They proudly boast about "doing their best work under pressure" and have cluttered desks with various piles of priorities—some of which they may never get to.

There are serious drawbacks to procrastination as we gain greater responsibilities. Waiting for that special last-minute signal to spur us into action may cause tremendous wear and tear on our bodies as the pressure to complete numerous tasks becomes too great. Often procrastinators think that

getting things done is only a matter of getting organized, but
they often put that off, too, and spend valuable time instead
beating themselves up with self-critical flogs.

### PRACTICE BECOMING A REAL-TIME SELF-CRITICIZER

Subscribers to real-time self-criticism use it as a way to keep
themselves in line. They will say things to themselves like:
"Don't get too cocky." "Don't think you're top dog. As soon
as you start thinking that way, someone will come along and
knock you down."

Grandmasters in chess subscribe to this usage of self-
criticism. *New York Times* writer Robert Byrne surprised his
readership when he told them that

> it is often thought that grandmasters rank among the
> world's great egotists, but generally that isn't so. To assure
> yourself of this, all you need to do is compliment one
> about a victory. Often the luminary's attention will all be
> on a move that turned out to be wrong.
>
> Don't think of this as grouchiness; rather, it is an effort
> to draw a lesson about what to avoid in the future.
> Dwelling on the clever tactics that won the game could
> gloss over what must be done to improve and thus spoil
> the central lesson of the game.
>
> Roman Dzindzichashvili's response to the praise he
> received after winning a game against Chicago's
> grandmaster, Dmitry Gurevich, exemplifies the ego pacer
> approach. "I should not have exchanged the light-square
> bishops," he said. Then, almost as an afterthought, he
> commented, "Oh, yes, the finish had some nice points."

## Hindsight self-criticism offers one of the best opportunities for learning

If it turns out that the source of the criticism is not an event (i.e., real-time self-criticism) but has its roots in longstanding bits of criticism, taking positive action may be considerably more difficult. Old tapes that play through a person's head— "Why can't you be smart like your older brother," "You are not glamorous looking so quit trying to dress or act like you are pretty"—cannot be pinned to a specific event and the value of the criticism is therefore questionable. How, for example, does one turn a criticism such as, "I'm so dumb," into positive action? The person could go out and get a college or graduate degree, but that's a lot of energy to spend for the purpose of eliminating self-doubt. That same person would most likely never forget the "D" they got in math on their way to the degree!

The point is that often we can be our own worst enemy and tell ourselves terrible things. Because we can't always control what we say to ourselves, it's important to invest energy in learning ways to handle the critical voice inside us.

At its best, self-criticism is a way to analyze oneself without interference by outsiders. No one has to know about the private conversations one has with oneself and the actions one intends to take. Included in this self-analysis is an examination of the motives behind one's actions. Self-criticism also serves as a vehicle for getting at our innermost thoughts and studying them in the hope of uncovering ways to improve ourselves.

Consequently, channeling self-criticism positively not only leads to increased motivation in the short run but also builds self-confidence, or the belief in oneself that is needed to pursue long-term goals or tasks.

Learning to effectively manage self-criticism is akin to learning to "be your own best friend," and it is a three-phase process. The three phases are: listening, validating the criticism, and assessing action.

### Listening

More often than not, when you engage in a self-critical dialogue, you're not really listening to what you're saying. You hear yourself, but it doesn't necessarily translate into inspecting what is being said. In order to inspect what is being said, get into the habit of *listening* to your internal dialogue. You won't stop the criticism, but you will objectify it and in the process minimize the "sting." To put it another way, the harsh, internal giver will stand aside and let the receiver take control.

### Validating the Criticism

In validating the criticism, you determine whether the information being transmitted is accurate, current, and specific. The best way to find all these things out is to ask questions such as

- Where is the information coming from and how old is it?
- Is it accurate?
- Is it specific?

These questions are modifications of questions in the receiver control chart in Chapter 5 and will help the self-criticizer gain valuable insights into his behavior.

**Managing the self-criticism process leads
to positive results and builds confidence**

### Assessing Action

During this phase it's valuable to ask the following questions:

- Do I want to do anything differently?
- What value is to be gained by taking action?
- What specifically can I do now?
- What specifically can I do differently next time?

The purpose of these questions is to determine whether action is warranted and, if so, what type. You may develop a preference for certain questions. The important thing to remember is that asking these or similar questions—and answering them—will empower you to effectively manage the self-criticism process and make it work for you.

Let's put this entire three-phase process into practice by examining two situations.

### *Situation 1*

Lee is head of sales for a medium-sized firm located in New Jersey. His boss suggested that he fly down south to meet with one of their vendors to explore the possibility of doing some joint business. Once the initial excitement wore off about what the joint venture could mean to the company, Lee got into his routine of self-doubt. Sitting at his desk, he said things to himself like: "You know you usually don't make a good first impression. Besides, when you speak, you tend to be too technical. These people are southerners, and they will probably be very uncomfortable with you. Chances are great you are going to be the one responsible for blowing this deal," and so forth. Sound familiar?

The first thing Lee has to do now is listen to what he is saying and remain neutral by interpreting what is being said as nothing more than "interesting information." He might begin with the statement: "Now let's investigate what I'm really saying." He could then ask himself "Where is this information coming from?" As obvious as it may seem to the observer, the person engaging in self-criticism is so wrapped up in the criticism that he doesn't see himself as the giver.

Lee needs to ask himself where he got the idea that he doesn't come across well to others. Was it in high school? Or did he poorly handle an encounter with someone at another job? What combination of events and factors led him to this conclusion? Lee may uncover a situation that he handled poorly four years ago when his former boss introduced him to a major client. After inspecting the past situation, Lee may quickly determine that he's criticizing himself unfairly. Nonetheless, he might ask himself whether any value can be gained from that experience that might help him when he goes to meet the vendor. Once he has considered the value of his ideas and whether to put them into action, Lee is ready to move on and direct his energies in productive ways.

### Situation 2

Marilyn is in the market development group of a California electronics manufacturing firm. At a recent staff meeting her boss, Jerry, is reviewing the status of a new project when he asks Marilyn a question pertinent to her area and she panics. Finally, in a state of total embarrassment, she claims she doesn't know.

As the meeting moves on to other agenda items, Marilyn is still stuck on the question she was unable to answer. Mentally she is beating herself up. "I'm so dumb!" she says to herself. "How could I not know the answer to his question?

I'm always the stupid one in the group. Here goes another round."

Like Lee, Marilyn needs to carefully listen to herself and remain neutral when inspecting the "information" she said about herself as the giver. For instance, whoever said she was dumb? Is the information accurate? In other words, Marilyn needs to inspect whether she is "always the stupid one in the group." Given the improbability of that being so, Marilyn's introspection should help her get at the root of the "old tapes" that are debilitating her. From there, she can go on to ask herself what she can do differently next time.

### Letting Go of Bad Feelings

No matter how effective you may become at managing and benefiting from self-criticism, sometimes there are nagging, negative feelings remaining that you can't seem to let go of. Two quick charges are particularly helpful in such circumstances.

The "audio cassette tape" quick charge will help you erase negative thoughts. First, mentally envision recording all your thoughts onto an audio cassette tape. Place your "recorded thoughts" into the cassette tape player and push the erase button. Instantly, your thoughts are eliminated. If you don't get the desired result the first time, repeat this quick charge.

The "so what" quick charge is also useful when you can't let go of negative feelings. Practicing the "so what" quick charge involves always using two steps. Step 1: Say to yourself, "So what—I made a mistake," or "So what—things didn't turn out as I had hoped." After you have identified everything that's upsetting you and have said "so what," you're ready for the next step. Step 2: Ask yourself what you are going to do about it. As you begin answering this question, specific ideas will start to form and energies will start to flow in a more positive direction as you develop a plan of action.

## WORRY AND GUILT

Worry and guilt are two emotions that need special attention. "Oh, stop worrying" and "You are always so guilt-ridden" are two of the common criticisms we give ourselves. It's useless, however, to try to deal with worry and guilt by giving yourself directives. For instance, have you ever stopped worrying after someone said to you, "Stop worrying"? A better idea than putting your energy into trying to stop worrying or feeling guilty is to put that energy into what you are thinking.

Ask yourself *what* you are worrying about. If it's an upcoming meeting, what about that meeting is causing you to worry? Is it that everyone in your group responsible for giving a presentation needs to be prepared and you are worried that one or two people may not be ready? Then ask if that worry is valid. And can you take action or do something about it? By asking yourself a series of questions, you can direct your energies in more productive ways. In essence, what you are doing is learning to *take action on your thinking, not on your emotions.* When you adopt this approach for managing worry, in essence you are acknowledging your feelings. Worrying acts as a signal notifying you that you need to delve further and seek out more specific information. Once you clarify what's causing you to worry, remember to examine whether it's controllable and lends itself to any immediate action.

Now let's talk about guilt. Is guilt bad? Absolutely not. You need guilt. Otherwise, what would stop you from making the same mistake twice?

Like other emotions, guilt needs to be managed. Too often we try to ignore our feelings of guilt, or we try to rationalize them away by saying to ourselves, "Oh, there's no need for feeling guilty. You didn't say or do anything wrong. The other person deserved it. He had it coming," and so on and so on. However, the feelings linger. At other times we hold back the guilt feelings in the hopes that they will disappear. But they never seem to. And when they reach an intolerable level, we take action—against our better instincts—solely for the purpose of minimizing the guilt!

Because guilt is so powerful, a good first step in managing it is to *validate* whether these feelings you are carrying around are justified. A subscriber of this approach is a woman psychologist and personal friend. As an author/lecturer, Dr. Gwendolyn Grant travels all over the United States making presentations on leadership and life skills development and assertiveness training. As a psychologist, Gwendolyn understands emotions—but that doesn't make her immune to feeling guilty, especially when she has been away from home too long. But as Gwendolyn always says, "If I am going to feel guilty—then it had better be for a just cause. So to determine whether my guilt feelings are valid, I'll ask my husband. Typically, I approach him by saying something like, 'Sweetheart, I'm feeling really guilty about being away from you too long—are my feelings justified?' Oftentimes, he will just look at me with his funny, yet familiar, expression—which quickly lets me know that I'm feeling guilty for no real reason."

So, whenever you are feeling guilty, take a tip from Gwendolyn and validate your feelings by going (whenever possible) directly to the source.


## CONCLUSION

Whenever you become the simultaneous giver and receiver of criticism, remember to listen to your internal dialogue, determine if what you are saying to yourself is valid (according to the day's events), and decide on what course of action needs to be taken.

When you listen to yourself and follow up with good questions, you are learning the basics of self-analysis, which, directed properly, can lead to self-improvement and increased motivation.

# The Relationship Expectation Model

■ How often have you been criticized about something you never thought was even a issue, let alone an important one? Think of occasions when you were criticized for not coming up to the expectations or standards of a manager, mate, or friend. You're not alone—we've all been there. Statements from receivers of criticism that reflect a conflict with givers' perceptions as to what level of performance was expected or what behavior was expected often take the form of: "Gee, don't blame me. I didn't know you wanted it done that way!" Or: "We never talked about that—how could you expect me to know?"

In cases where there is confusion about expectations or even an absence of expectations between a giver and a receiver, there is a very good chance that criticism will be the communication device that uncovers the mixed signals or the lack of congruency of perceived expectations. Although it may at first appear to be a somewhat elaborate way of ensuring a congruency of expectations between manager and employee or husband and wife, the relationship expectation model (see page 106) can easily assess a relationship and provide valuable insights to both parties.

The model is a visual representation of key areas in a relationship between people whose intention it is to engage in a cooperative effort. It has applications to the work environment as well as the home environment. At work, managers can use the relationship expectation model for developmental purposes to help identify areas in which misunderstandings or differences exist within the relationship. In all relationships, it can serve as a catalyst of mutual understanding. When used properly, the model is an excellent way of avoiding doing damage to a relationship through unproductive dialogues couched in negatives.

## AREAS IN THE RELATIONSHIP EXPECTATION MODEL

Ideally, the relationship expectation model should be limited as an exercise between two people who wish to uncover various perceptions of their mutual understanding of expectations as they relate to the accomplishment of a common objective.

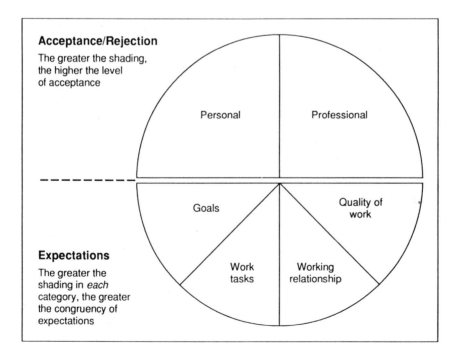

**Acceptance/Rejection**
The greater the shading, the higher the level of acceptance

Personal

Professional

Goals

Quality of work

**Expectations**
The greater the shading in *each* category, the greater the congruency of expectations

Work tasks

Working relationship

The lower half of the model defines a working relationship in terms of expectations established in four general zones:

**Goals** Includes individual personal goals, departmental goals, and organizational goals.

**Work tasks** Examines whether responsibilities and work assignments have been clearly established and whether the role of each party is understood by both parties.

**Quality of work** Encompasses having a clear understanding of what quality means in regards to established personal standards as well as standards set by the organization. Knowing what to do is not enough.

**Working relationship** Explores the perceived level of understanding that exists in regard to how best to communicate and work cooperatively together. This includes knowing individual criticism preferences and meaningful ways to give praise and recognition.

The upper half of the model visually represents a relationship in terms of personal and professional acceptance or respect for one another. The professional profile considers important aspects of a relationship such as perceptions of competency, fairness, honesty, loyalty, ethical practices, dress and mannerisms, and technical proficiency. The personal profile describes how well one knows another outside of the job environment—where there's no pressure to meet deadlines and where there's an absence of the need to ensure consistent work quality. It's the distinction that one often hears from a co-worker or mate: "He is completely different when he is away from the job," or "He's a great guy when he's not at work."

## PUTTING THE MODEL TO WORK

Again, the model is designed to be a visual comparison of perceptions between two people with regard to their mutual understanding of cooperative matters such as goals, quality of the working relationship, respect for work quality, and work tasks in general, as well as a comparison of shared levels of personal and professional acceptance or mutual respect. To use the model it is advisable to begin with the elements in the lower half, because expectations greatly impact the quality of the relationship and the cooperative spirit developed.

### How to Complete the Lower Half of the Model

To complete the model, individual parties to the relationship can either privately shade in areas as appropriate and compare the results upon completion, or the model can be shaded in together. Either way will work to your mutual benefit.

### *Step 1—Shading in the Model*

Using a pen or colored pencil, shade in the level of understanding that exists in the relationship, as you see it, in regard to each of the four zones: goals, work tasks, quality of work, and working relationship. Approximate the clarity of your mutual understanding of these factors by completely filling in a zone to reflect total mutual understanding or partially filling in a zone to indicate a lesser degree of total mutual understanding.

**Goals**  Starting at the center of the circle, shade in the degree to which goals have been openly discussed, are mutually understood, and are consistently adhered to.

**Work tasks**  The degree to which work task expectations have been clearly communicated and understood is represented by the amount of shading in the work tasks zone. Indicate the degree of understanding that exists by following the same approach used when shading the goal zone.

**Quality of work**  Expectations involving respect for work quality are oftentimes assumed. Shade in this zone according to the degree of clear understanding that exists within the relationship in regard to work quality issues. Remember, start shading in from the center of the circle.

**Working relationship**  Is there a clear understanding of how mistakes will be addressed and, when outstanding work is performed, how it will be recognized? Starting at the center of the circle, shade in the degree of understanding that exists in regard to the working relationship.

### Step II—Comparing Models

If the shading described above is done individually, both parties next compare models, noting where differences and similarities appear.

### Step III—Interpretation of the Model

The amount of shading covering each zone represents a visual measure of whether expectations have been clearly communicated and understood. The greater the shading, the more expectations are congruent, or understood and agreed upon. When congruency of expectations exists within the relationship, there will be less time wasted on critical dialogue and more time spent on like-minded productivity.

Concurrently, when there is congruency within a working relationship zone, receivers will be more receptive to criticism and more willing to take action in that specific zone area.

### Step IV—Engaging in a Dialogue

Identify a zone that has been shaded in less than other zones or where differences in the amount of shading appear. Select one of these particular zones to discuss first. The best way to engage in a productive dialogue is to ask open-ended questions related to the zone. For instance, if one party shaded in half of the quality of work zone on their model while the other party shaded in this zone completely, a dialogue might be initiated by the party who shaded in their zone completely. A good opening comment might be: "It appears we have a different perception about the quality expectations of the job. Would you like me to comment?" The purpose of the discussion is to establish an understanding and to reach an agreement on how best to work together. The focus of the conversation should not be on who's right or who's wrong. To avoid letting the conversation deteriorate, both parties need to "listen to understand," as opposed to "listening to judge."

### Step V—Establishing New Understandings

In order to develop mutual expectations, negotiating and compromising may be a necessary part of the exchange.

Once an understanding has been reached it is important that it be kept up, that is, managed and consistently followed.

## How to Complete the Upper Half of the Model

Completing the upper half of the model should be done selectively because discussing professional and personal levels of acceptance is a very sensitive zone. While addressing this zone may be sensitive, avoiding it doesn't negate its existence. Employees, bosses, co-workers, mates, and friends, for that matter, regularly assess the quality of relationships in terms of acceptance or respect for one another. The upper half of the model allows such assessment to become mutually clear.

### Step I—Shading in the Model

Complete the model privately, or do it jointly with the other person. As described above, shade in the degree of personal and professional acceptance perceived within the relationship using a pen or colored pencil.

### Step II—Comparing the Models

If the model was colored in by each party separately, compare the two models by looking for similarities and differences in the degree of shading applied.

### Step III—Interpreting the Upper Half of the Model

Where congruency exists, acceptance levels match. The more the shading matches, the higher the level of acceptance. Professional and personal acceptance levels may vary without greatly damaging the ability to work effectively together. For example, people can feel more acceptance of others professionally than they do personally. The shading would indicate this difference by covering a greater amount of the professional zone than the personal one. This might likely be the case in technical environments where individuals working together might not necessarily like one another, but will cooperate and work together effectively because of the high degree of technical expertise they bring to the overall effort. If both parties color in only a small portion of the acceptance zone, or if major differences in perception exist in each of these zones, then the relationship shows strain. Greater energy invariably needs to be invested to keep a cooperative and productive relationship going. The model originally depicted as a perfect circle divided in half would change shape, as different zones would become more pronounced than others.

### Step IV—Engaging in a Dialogue

When engaging in a dialogue, begin by focusing on zones where you both match or where there is congruency of expectations. Explore what factors contributed to the similar shading. Where there are differences, discuss what contributes to these differences of perception.

For example, a boss and his newly transferred employee went through this exercise. In the professional acceptance zone, the employee had only colored in a small portion of the zone, whereas the boss had shaded in a larger portion. This led to discussion that resulted in further strengthening their relationship. The employee learned about his boss's background and his extensive work experience in the zone he was managing. This newly discovered information helped the employee gain more respect for his boss. It's important to keep the purpose of the dialogue—to develop mutual understanding—clearly in focus.

## CONCLUSION

The relationship expectation model is a useful tool for visually representing a relationship between people who are interested in working cooperatively together. The model functions as an excellent catalyst for opening lines of communication in a nonrestrictive manner.

With managers and employees, the model can serve as a valuable developmental tool that will not only be helpful in avoiding reasons for criticism, but will also enrich the productivity of the working relationship.

Finally, it is important to keep in mind that relationships, like so many other things in life, change over time. We adopt new values, revise our perceptions, and gain new insights into how things can be done better. All of this revisionary thinking will inevitably alter relationships, whether with mates, co-workers, or friends. To that end, it would be worthwhile to apply the relationship model periodically in order to audit understandings, expectations, and perceptions.

# Giver Eloquence Questionnaire

■ We are often unaware of how we come across to others when delivering criticism. We can depend on the fact that few people will be open enough to let us know what they really think. In fact, findings from a wealth of interviews consistently confirm that most employees feel that it's not the criticism that's troublesome, but how it is delivered that's upsetting and hard to take. Lack of eloquence in delivering the criticism message, therefore, can turn the best intentioned message into a devastating experience for all involved.

The giver eloquence questionnaire is designed to assess your overall effectiveness when delivering criticism. Allow yourself fifteen to thirty days to put the ideas and skill sets discussed in the manual into practice before retaking the questionnaire. Note any progress and, if necessary, develop an action plan similar to the one outlined in Appendix C to help you improve your effectiveness when delivering criticism.

## Directions

Take a few minutes by yourself to answer each of the following questions by checking the most appropriate response. It's important to carefully consider each question and give an honest response. This will help in determining how eloquent you are when delivering criticism.

|  | Amost never | Rarely | Sometimes | Frequently | Almost always |
|---|---|---|---|---|---|

## Questions

1. When you deliver criticism, do you later regret some of the things said? ☐ ☐ ☐ ☐ ☐

2. After delivering criticism, do you spend extra time clarifying what you meant? ☐ ☐ ☐ ☐ ☐

3. When you criticize, do receivers typically respond defensively? ☐ ☐ ☐ ☐ ☐

4. After delivering criticism, is there typically very little conversation between yourself and the receiver? ☐ ☐ ☐ ☐ ☐

5. After you criticize, do receivers fail to take action? ☐ ☐ ☐ ☐ ☐

6. When you criticize, do receivers make comments about "how" the criticism is delivered (e.g., "stop yelling," "take it easy," "let's not blow this thing out of proportion, I've made a mistake and nothing more," "calm down")? ☐ ☐ ☐ ☐ ☐

7. Do receivers want to discuss matters further, but there is rarely enough time? ☐ ☐ ☐ ☐ ☐

8. When receivers ask for specific examples, are you unable to provide them? ☐ ☐ ☐ ☐ ☐

9. Do you find that specific examples cited are not consistent with the criticism being delivered? ☐ ☐ ☐ ☐ ☐

|  | Amost never | Rarely | Sometimes | Frequently | Almost always |
|---|---|---|---|---|---|
| 10. After you deliver criticism, are receivers unwilling to act on the criticism in a timely manner? | ☐ | ☐ | ☐ | ☐ | ☐ |
| 11. Do you forget to follow up with the receiver after he has taken corrective action? | ☐ | ☐ | ☐ | ☐ | ☐ |
| 12. Does the receiver fail to understand the criticism? | ☐ | ☐ | ☐ | ☐ | ☐ |
| 13. When you deliver criticism, do you lack a clear idea of the behavior you want from the receiver? | ☐ | ☐ | ☐ | ☐ | ☐ |
| 14. Do you deliver criticism that cannot be acted upon by the receiver? | ☐ | ☐ | ☐ | ☐ | ☐ |
| 15. Do receivers make comments about how bad the timing of the criticism is (e.g., "gosh, you are hitting me at a bad time," "I've had such a bad day, can this wait until later")? | ☐ | ☐ | ☐ | ☐ | ☐ |
| 16. Do you criticize others when you are upset or in a hurry? | ☐ | ☐ | ☐ | ☐ | ☐ |
| 17. Do receivers say "stop yelling at me" when you are not raising your voice? | ☐ | ☐ | ☐ | ☐ | ☐ |
| 18. Prior to delivering criticism, do you fail to consider whether you are the appropriate person? | ☐ | ☐ | ☐ | ☐ | ☐ |
| 19. Do you present criticism for what it is and let the receiver determine whether or not there is any value? | ☐ | ☐ | ☐ | ☐ | ☐ |
| 20. Do you leave it up to the receiver to develop appropriate actions to take? | ☐ | ☐ | ☐ | ☐ | ☐ |

|  | Amost never | Rarely | Sometimes | Frequently | Almost always |
|---|---|---|---|---|---|
| 21. Do you avoid taking steps to ensure that you let the receiver know you believe in her? | ☐ | ☐ | ☐ | ☐ | ☐ |
| 22. Does the receiver resist your criticism by saying "no one ever told me..."? | ☐ | ☐ | ☐ | ☐ | ☐ |
| 23. Do you formulate your words and message at the same time you are delivering the criticism? | ☐ | ☐ | ☐ | ☐ | ☐ |
| 24. Do you deliver criticism without taking into account the individual's criticism preference? | ☐ | ☐ | ☐ | ☐ | ☐ |
| 25. Do you criticize others in public? | ☐ | ☐ | ☐ | ☐ | ☐ |
| 26. Do past criticisms recur in subsequent conversations? | ☐ | ☐ | ☐ | ☐ | ☐ |

## Scoring yourself

In the matrix at the top of the next page, write in column 2 the number of times that you checked each of the five possible answers. Multiply the numbers you enter by the factors in column 3, and enter the results in column 4. To find your score, add together the five numbers in column 4.

| (1) | (2) Number of | (3) | (4) |
|---|---|---|---|
| Answer | Answers | Multiply by | Totals |
| Almost never | _____ | 1 | _____ |
| Rarely | _____ | 2 | _____ |
| Sometimes | _____ | 3 | _____ |
| Frequently | _____ | 4 | _____ |
| Almost always | _____ | 5 | _____ |
| | | TOTAL SCORE | _____ |

### *Interpreting your score value*

**35 and below**  If your total score value falls in this range, then you have perfected the art of giving quality criticism. Besides ensuring that you continue to put into practice what you know, it might be helpful if you shared your insights and knowledge with others.

**36–45**  If your total score value falls in this range, then you are close to delivering criticism with eloquence. Carefully review your responses to each of the questions to see if any pattern emerges that will help you better focus on areas to refine. Concentrate on one area that needs work and practice for at least a two-week period. When implementation takes less effort, then move to another area that needs work.

**46–55** If your total score value falls in this range, then it is advisable to reread Chapter 3. Also, make sure you *think* before delivering criticism. For the next two weeks, rather than launch into the criticism, plan on purposely delaying what you have to say. And make sure you ask yourself, "What's your purpose?"

**56 and above**   If your score value is 56 or over, then it is important for you to reread Chapters 1, 2 and 3. If you find you must criticize, be sure to pull out the giver methodology chart (Chapter 3) and use it as a reference. It might be helpful, as you master the skill of delivering quality criticism, to hand the receiver control chart (Chapter 5) to the receiver of criticism. Let her help you as you work to sharpen your skills in giving criticism.

# Giver Action Plan

■     The giver action plan is a short questionnaire designed to be used while preparing to deliver criticism to help you better work through a difficult situation. This plan will help sort things out by walking you through a series of questions that parallel the giver methodology chart. During the mental rehearsal step you will be asked specific questions to help you determine whether you are properly prepared to deliver criticism. Lastly, the giver action plan enables you to assess the outcome of the criticism exchange (Part III).

To use this form, first complete Parts I and II privately prior to delivering criticism. Once the criticism exchange has taken place, return to Part III of this form to assess your effectiveness and the final outcome.

## GIVER ACTION PLAN SHEET

### Part 1: Identification Of Situation

    1. State the situation as it presently exists.


    2. Identify the criticism categories that best represent the situation described above. (Use a check (✔) in the space provided to identify the category.)

        ☐ Personal style

        ☐ Compatibility with peers, subordinates, and/or superiors

        ☐ Quality service

☐ Work performance quality

☐ Work responsibility

☐ Judgment

3. What is your relationship to the person?


4. How do you typically make contact with this person? (Use a check (✔) to indicate your answer.)

☐ In person      ☐ By phone      ☐ In writing

• Of the three approaches suggested above, which is most effective? (Circle your answer)


## Part II: Preparation Phase

Before delivering the criticism, be sure you can answer the following questions.

1. Do you know what behavior you want from the person? Be specific.


• Is the person capable of delivering this behavior? Detail evidence to support your conclusion.


• If you are unsure whether the person can deliver the desired behavior, what steps will you take to gather information?

2. Do you know how the person prefers to be criticized? Describe.

- If you are unsure of how the person prefers to be criticized, what steps will you take to find out?

3. What individual and mutual goals can the criticism or desired action be linked to?

4. Can you identify specific examples to help validate the criticism? (If not, delay criticizing until you can.)

5. To increase the receiver's level of understanding and acceptance of the criticism, what concepts can you use when communicating with this person?

- If unsure, what steps will you take to find out?

6. How does the person predominantly sense his environment? (Check most appropriate choice.) If you are unsure, it's best to find out. Knowing this helps to enhance communication.

☐ Auditory (hear)                ☐ Olfactory (smell)

☐ Kinesthetic (feel)            ☐ Gustatory (taste)

☐ Visual (see)

7. To ensure acceptance of the criticism, how can you present it so that it will be perceived as having value?

8. What steps can you take to ensure that the criticism will not be taken personally? (If unsure, delay the criticism.)

9. Do you want to mutually discuss and develop a "follow-up" plan to monitor actions taken?

10. Do you want to discuss consequences?

11. Review mentally how to deliver the criticism. Did you consider all of the following?

☐ Past history          ☐ Tone of voice
☐ Listening            ☐ Timing
☐ Handling emotions     ☐ Appropriate person
☐ Staying focused       ☐ Manner of style and
☐ Specific word choices    delivery

If you failed to consider any of the above, take the time to review that aspect of giving criticism and ensure that the delivery is effective.

## Part III: Giver Success Assessment

Because giving criticism is a skill, it is helpful to "critique" yourself after delivering criticism to others. The following rating form will help you in your assessment.

### *Directions*

Identify how effective you were at implementing each of the items below, using the scale provided.

| Delivery | Not very effectively | Somewhat effectively | Effectively | Very effectively |
|---|---|---|---|---|
| Clearly communicated specific desired behavior | ☐ | ☐ | ☐ | ☐ |
| Communicated criticism consistently with person's preference | ☐ | ☐ | ☐ | ☐ |
| Linked criticism to individual or mutually shared goals | ☐ | ☐ | ☐ | ☐ |
| Provided specific examples | ☐ | ☐ | ☐ | ☐ |
| Used appropriate language to increase understandability | ☐ | ☐ | ☐ | ☐ |
| Criticism communicated as clearly in bounds | ☐ | ☐ | ☐ | ☐ |
| Considered timing | ☐ | ☐ | ☐ | ☐ |
| Determined if I was appropriate person to deliver criticism | ☐ | ☐ | ☐ | ☐ |
| Listened | ☐ | ☐ | ☐ | ☐ |

| Delivery | Not very effectively | Somewhat effectively | Effectively | Very effectively |
|---|---|---|---|---|
| Handled emotions | ☐ | ☐ | ☐ | ☐ |
| Remained properly focused on issue at hand | ☐ | ☐ | ☐ | ☐ |

## Part IV: Giver Outcome Assessment

| Outcome | Not very sure | Somewhat sure | Sure | Very sure |
|---|---|---|---|---|
| Criticism received as intended | ☐ | ☐ | ☐ | ☐ |
| Reached an agreement on desired action | ☐ | ☐ | ☐ | ☐ |
| Relationship strengthened | ☐ | ☐ | ☐ | ☐ |
| Person genuinely willing to take action | ☐ | ☐ | ☐ | ☐ |
| Follow-up measures developed | ☐ | ☐ | ☐ | ☐ |

# Goal Sheet for Perfecting the Art of Giving Criticism

■ The goal sheet on the following pages can assist you in developing a more effective criticism style, through integrating the skill sets and insights presented throughout this manual. Use the goal sheet to identify specific techniques for improvement, or to focus on a particular (or repetitive) situation in which you want to enhance your performance in giving criticism. The goal sheet can also provide a valuable scorecard for periodic self-appraisal in which you re-evaluate your performance overall or in certain key areas. By returning to prior self-evaluations, you not only measure your growth in the art of giving effective criticism, but also enjoy a rewarding experience in the equally important art of self-criticism.

My objective is to focus on:

| | Date started | Date completed | Directed at whom | Mid-point progress check* | Level of overall success* |
|---|---|---|---|---|---|
| **Establishing Expectations** | | | | | |
| ☐ Building clearer work task expectations | | | | | |
| ☐ Identifying work quality expectations | | | | | |
| ☐ Clarifying how best to work together | | | | | |
| ☐ Re-establishing a clear understanding of goals | | | | | |
| **Giving Criticism More Eloquently** | | | | | |
| ☐ Thinking before delivering criticism | | | | | |
| ☐ Identifying specific desired behaviors prior to delivering criticism | | | | | |
| ☐ Making more time to engage in a meaningful dialogue | | | | | |
| ☐ Providing more specific examples | | | | | |
| ☐ Presenting the criticism so it's perceived as having value | | | | | |
| ☐ Listening with patience | | | | | |

☐ Paying more attention to my tone of voice

## Using Control More Effectively When Receiving Criticism

☐ Listening to understand vs. listening to judge

☐ Being less defensive

☐ Asking more questions to validate criticism

☐ Avoiding the tendency to personalize criticism

☐ Exposing the intentions behind criticism

☐ Making sure I understand the specific desired action

## Self-Criticism

☐ Listening to self more objectively

☐ Validating statements by asking key questions

☐ Using quick charges for regaining self-control

☐ Being sure to explore specific courses of action to take

* Develop your own criteria or set of expectations before completing.

Deborah Bright is the president of Bright Enterprises, Inc., a New York–based resource company specializing in improving performance and enhancing the quality of management. Among her clients are the FBI, where she helps train law enforcement officers from around the world; MCI, where she trains all new senior managers; IBM, where she conducted several management training sessions; and also the Professional Golfer's Association of America, where she trains professional golfers in enhancing personal effectiveness. Deborah Bright is currently presenting tailored programs to firms such as the Young Presidents Organizations, IBM, and Continental Cablevision.

In addition to conducting training programs as a part of the Bright Learning Center, Deborah Bright is the author of the best-seller, *Creative Relaxation: Turning Your Stress Into Positive Energy.* "Creative relaxation" is a program that she discovered and developed to help people handle pressure and direct it in more positive ways. A sixty-minute audio-cassette tape based on the same book is available in bookstores nationwide. She has also written *Gearing Up for the Fast Lane: New Tools for Management in a High-Tech World* and her latest achievement, her new book on criticism, *Criticism In Your Life: How to Give It, How to Take It, How To Make It Work for You.* This book takes a definitive look at how to handle and successfully work with the giving and taking of criticism. Soon to be released is an audio-cassette tape album on using criticism as a motivator. It features Steve Allen, Jane Meadows, and Dr. Bright.

An unpublicized aspect of Deborah Bright's work is training amateur and professional athletes, such as members of the U.S. Tennis Association and the Detroit Tigers, with a focus on maximizing their performance in highly competitive situations. Dr. Bright was once ranked among the top ten U.S. women divers, and her impressive career in platform and springboard competition led her to the Olympic Trials.

Deborah Bright earned her doctorate in adult education from Arizona State University and is a member of the faculty at New York University where, as an adjunct professor, she teaches courses on "Turning Job Stress Into Positive Energy" and "Managing for Exceptional Performance." She is also a contributing columnist to the *New York Law Journal* and *The National Law Journal*.